Martha's Vineyard IN THE ROARING TWENTIES

Radicals & Rascals

THOMAS DRESSER

Foreword by Chris Baer, author of "This Was Then" column in the *Martha's Vineyard Times*

Published by The History Press
Charleston, SC
www.historypress.com

Front cover, top: Odd fellows. *Courtesy of the Martha's Vineyard Museum*; *bottom*: The Triad Club. *Courtesy of the Martha's Vineyard Museum.*
Back cover: The Tivoli. *Courtesy of the Martha's Vineyard Museum.*

First published 2023

Manufactured in the United States

ISBN 9781467152662

Library of Congress Control Number: 2022950076

CONTENTS

Contents

FOREWORD

The stretch of twentieth century between the end of the first World War and the beginning of the Great Depression had a lot going on. It was the era of radio, flappers, jazz, silent films, and biplanes. Of Prohibition and its local flip side: rumrunning. It encompassed the waning years of Azorean immigration and the sparks that ignited Oak Bluffs into a transformative Black summer community. The beginning of the State Forest and the last days of the heath hen. The end of a global pandemic and the beginning of a financial collapse.

I honestly don't remember how I met Tom Dresser; I feel like I've always known him. He is a former elementary school teacher, and he fits the role: patient, smiling, welcoming, kind, comfortable, and—perhaps most relevant here—a straightforward, down-to-earth explainer of an incredibly broad selection of complex topics.

Some of Tom's stories here are uniquely local—like the tale of the opportunists who looted the *Port Hunter*, providing a generation with leather jackets, scratchy underwear, and candles. Others—on pandemics, politics, law, and war—are national or global in scope (and perhaps prescient of echoed issues we face in the 2020s). Tom's tales are well stocked with colorful characters—Frank Butler chased by Coast Guard machine-gunners, for instance, or the political radicals holing up in a Chilmark farmhouse—and he tackles not just the light-hearted but the tragic stories as well, like the brutal John Dwight massacre of 1923.

Tom Dresser is no rascal, even if he is a bit of a rebel. He's the most prolific author on Vineyard history in Vineyard history and perhaps in any genre; he has something like sixteen books and counting on Island history alone. (I've lost count, even as they weigh down one whole shelf in my office.)

Tom is a literary jack-of-all-trades, effortlessly switching his focus from music to fashion to war to religion, literature, crime, shipwrecks, race, and gender, with enviable ease. One minute he zooms in to visit familiar people and local shops, and the next minute he zooms out to examine international trends.

The thing about Tom is that he does his homework. As smooth as his prose reads, it's backed by an enormous amount of research. Too many historical writers fiddle with the truth to fit a nostalgic narrative or make great deductive leaps to bridge a chasm of missing information, but Tom's work you can take to the bank. I am honored I could provide a few background tidbits and photos for this important work, but in doing so I can also attest to his painstaking, behind-the-scenes labors.

I am forever indebted to Tom for the morning he invited me to join him for a leisurely coffee on the porch of his tidy cottage on East Chop. I wanted to write a book. He had lots of hard-earned advice, and that morning he shared all of it. But like a good teacher, he stopped short of telling me what to do. He laid out my options, carefully described the benefits and pitfalls of each, and wished me well. Within the year, my book *Martha's Vineyard Tales* would be published, but it wouldn't have happened without Tom's help.

I remember being surprised to learn that Tom worked part time as a school bus driver on the Island. What was this prolific historical author doing driving Bus #119 for thirteen years? I assume it was because he enjoyed the job—the kids loved him and were upset when he retired. But I can also imagine that in driving across the Island every morning, Tom had a unique opportunity to ponder the rich history of Martha's Vineyard across the spans of both time and space.

So, get excited! It's time to hop on Tom's bus and let him take us on a tour of a unique island during a unique era. He has a lot of curious stops for us ahead.

Chris Baer
Author of "This Was Then" column in the *MV Times*
Author of *Martha's Vineyard Tales*
April 2022

PROLOGUE

The decade between the end of the First World War and the beginning of the Great Depression constitutes the Roaring Twenties. Its effects were felt in varying degrees across the country and around the world. Many of the measures enacted then are felt in today's world, a century later. While a lot has changed since the 1920s, a good deal remains a focus of life today. Think COVID-19, the right to vote, Prohibition, immigration restrictions, critical race theory, and fears of Communism

This is the story of that remarkable decade and how it unfolded on Martha's Vineyard.

When I began work on this book in early January 2022, I assumed my effort would be chronological, beginning with 1920 and concluding in 1930, the conventional view of sequential history: start at the beginning and end at the end.

After a month of reading, researching, and writing, I realized this was a story to be told in an unconventional manner. Basically, everything that stood for anything in the 1920s was happening simultaneously. And to understand this unique decade in American history, we must grasp it whole, like the bloomin' onion served at Outback Steakhouse. Each petal, each major topic, is part of the whole to be experienced relative to everything else. No single event stands alone.

The years of the 1920s were filled with a range of events, experiences, fears, laws, and advances that affected Martha's Vineyard. Prohibition. Women's right to vote. The Red Scare. The Harlem Renaissance. Immigration.

Radio. Airplanes. The Spanish flu. Each topic deserves its own chapter, but they overlap and intersect, time and again. Hence, you can read this book by topic or random chapters, rather than front to back. However you choose to tackle the 1920s, you should be fully apprised of the influence of the Roaring Twenties on Martha's Vineyard by the time you reach the epilogue.

Granted, national events did occur at a specific date; their influence permeated the whole decade. The Black Sox Scandal, 1919. The Tulsa Race Massacre, 1921. Teapot Dome, 1923. The Scopes Trial, 1925. Lindbergh's flight, 1927. The decade ended with the Wall Street crash in 1929. These national events occurred within the social, political, economic, and cultural confines that had an impact on and influenced the Roaring 1920s. This is the story of that decade as it played out on Martha's Vineyard, as the United States was emerging from the war to end all wars and blindly heading straight into the Great Depression.

The sinking of the supply ship *Port Hunter* off Martha's Vineyard on November 2, 1918, preceded the signing of the Armistice on November 11, 1918, which effectively ended the First World War. The *Port Hunter* sank off East Chop, and after the crew was rescued, the ship was scavenged by Vineyarders eager to purloin woolen underwear or steal trench candles. A week later, the war was over, and patriotic Vineyarders paraded down Main Street Edgartown. These two public activities, one illegal, the other patriotic, were accepted as normal by fellow Vineyarders. The sunken ship offered the opportunity to make a quick buck or score a cool army jacket. The Armistice was a time to celebrate, to party and live beyond the reaches of war. The conflicting consciences of local Islanders mirrored the complex social scene that spread across America. The 1920s roared into Martha's Vineyard just like everywhere else.

Dorothy West wrote descriptively about Martha's Vineyard in the Roaring Twenties. Her words capture the atmosphere to the point you can almost smell the excitement in the air:

> *The twenties were in giant-size bloom on the Island. Summer money fell like rain on all the towns, especially the down-Island towns, and notably Oak Bluffs, with its accessibility to steamboat landings, with its carriages and automobiles for hire, its Tivoli dance hall, its moving-picture houses, its*

> *bandstand in the park, and the Methodist Tabernacle, no longer a hotbed of fiery evangelists, but still an impressive place of assembly, with important guest speakers on a latitude of topics, and musical performances with gifted artists, and the magical, lantern-lit Illumination Night, as unique an experience as can be had.*[1]

The Roaring Twenties barreled across the Island.

ACKNOWLEDGEMENTS

When I shared the idea of writing about the Roaring Twenties, my daughter Amy excitedly drew parallels between then and now and wondered if the 2020s will end the way the 1920s did.

Chris Baer was a great help writing the foreword and sharing multiple images. His "This Was Then" columns in the *MV Times* are filled full of fun facts from Vineyard history. His assistance in this project was payback for my encouragement for him to pursue his *Martha's Vineyard Tales*. His book captures many unusual historical anecdotes he has uncovered over the years.

Bow Van Riper at the Martha's Vineyard Museum is always ready to offer an item of historical relevance, as well as a store of Island photos.

Hilary Wallcox of the *Vineyard Gazette* was most generous with her time and curiosity in the topic at hand; much of my research focused on *Gazette* articles from the 1920s. Hilary encouraged me to access the *Gazette*'s Time Machine, which was a welcome treat. And she's great at locating missing details to arcane stories.

Donna Leon and Susan Phillips of Phillips Hardware graciously shared stories and images of their century-old store on Circuit Avenue.

Amelia Smith added a human-interest element with her ancestor's book on the Woollcott family.

Eddie Bendavid shared a bit about Jim's Package Store.

Joan Boyken of MV Obsession willingly shared her mother's fashion statement from a century ago.

And Lianne Archer diligently tried to assist my search for the Vineyard Trust.

My thanks to the staff of the Oak Bluffs Library, always friendly and capable in meeting my needs.

For more tales of illicit alcohol adventures, I recommend Everett Allen's *Black Ships: Rumrunners of Prohibition*.

The History Press has stood behind my work for fifteen years, through fifteen books. Once more, Mike Kinsella came through, approving my topic and suggesting how to improve it. Thanks.

Senior copy editor Abigail Fleming once again did a superb job editing my manuscript, even allowing me to use the Oxford comma, which we both value.

And Dani McGrath stands ready to promote, advocate, and advance my literary projects.

My deepest thanks go to my life partner, Joyce. She carefully edited each chapter and conscientiously offered suggestions to improve the quality of the work. Her photographs enliven the pages throughout.

This book is dedicated to the people of Ukraine.

1
WAR

The United States entered the First World War on April 4, 1917. Across Martha's Vineyard, young men volunteered to serve. It was a matter of national pride, a chance to support our allies overseas, and a sense of responsibility that encouraged young men to volunteer.

In Massachusetts, a contest was held to see which town would have the highest percentage of its male population volunteer to join the army.

Gay Head, a tiny town in the southwest corner of Martha's Vineyard, won the contest. "All able-bodied men volunteered to serve," June Manning proudly announced, as reported in a 2015 article in the *Vineyard Gazette*. Her grandfather Walter W. Manning was one of those men who went to war. "There were 23 men who served. Only one of them didn't come home; George Belain didn't come home."[2]

Gay Head had the highest percentage of volunteers for its population of any town in the state of Massachusetts. To recognize and honor this impressive show of patriotism, Governor Samuel McCall and his Lieutenant Governor Calvin Coolidge visited the Vineyard on July 13, 1918. A grand parade, boasting more than 170 floats and decorated cars, slowly made its way across the Vineyard, a procession "that wound its way over the splendid state roads, past the gaily decked buildings and hedgerows of the towns and even of the most remote and isolated nooks and crannies of the island."[3]

Reporter Steve Myrick captured the excitement in an article nearly a century later: "It was the day of the annual powwow in Gay Head. Gathered for the dedication were Native Americans in traditional tribal dress, side by side with men in suits and women in colorful summer dresses." That was fitting, as the volunteers were primarily of Native descent, celebrating the festivity of the powwow.

"Among the speakers that day," noted Myrick, "was Edwin D. Vanderhoop, a Civil War veteran who later represented Martha's Vineyard in the state legislature. His son, Leonard F. Vanderhoop, was one of four members of the extended family who volunteered for service in World War I." Grandson Durwood "Woody" Vanderhoop recalled his grandfather's injuries in the war but also the pride of having served in the military for his town and country.

Elsie Diamond presented the symbolic key of Gay Head to Governor McCall. Today, a plaque honoring the Gay Head volunteers stands proudly by the town offices of Aquinnah, formerly Gay Head. The patina on the plaque reflects the dedication and patriotism exhibited by two dozen Native Americans who volunteered in the First World War.

Other Island towns sent volunteers: 81 men enlisted from Vineyard Haven, Oak Bluffs sent 50 men, 45 men volunteered from Edgartown, Gay Head counted 23 volunteers, West Tisbury sent 14 men, and Chilmark sent 7 soldiers off to war. All the Island towns recognized the 220 brave souls who volunteered their services.

The number of civilian and military casualties in the First World War was staggering. Sixteen million people died; another twenty-one million people were injured.

The sixteen million deaths included nearly seven million civilians, primarily in France and Germany. The United States, and our Allies, also known as the Entente Powers, lost nearly six million soldiers; the Central Powers lost over three million.

Martha's Vineyard was not immune to the tragedy of war. Two young men, one from Gay Head, the other from Vineyard Haven, did not return from the war. George Belain and George Freudenberger both died overseas, not on the battlefield, but in the hospital, months after the war was over.

Disease could be as devastating as injury in warfare.

Private George Belain served in the 77th Division, 306th Field Artillery Regiment. He succumbed to disease on February 13, 1919, a few months

Judge Beriah T. Hillman, a Civil War veteran, posed with World War I veterans at the Edgartown memorial on Pease Point Way. *Courtesy of the Martha's Vineyard Museum.*

The plaque at Oak Grove Cemetery in Vineyard Haven honors World War I veterans. Each year, a wreath is placed on the plaque on Memorial Day. *Photo by Joyce Dresser.*

after the war was over. Belain was buried in the Army Battle Monuments Commission location Plot B, Row 9, Grave 16 at St. Mihiel, the American Cemetery in Thiaucourt, France. He was awarded the World War I Victory Medal.

Private George Freudenberger was also a casualty of the First World War. He was listed as a resident of Vineyard Haven by HonorStates.org, a veterans' memorial organization. Private Freudenberger died on February 3, 1919, in France. Freudenberger was awarded the World War I Victory Medal posthumously.

We know something of George Freudenberger's relatives. He had a younger sister named Adelaide Freudenberger Davis and a brother, Franklin. At twenty-three, Franklin changed his last name to Howell, the siblings' mother's maiden name.

Private Freudenberger left a young wife, Margaret Finnegan, and a daughter, Helen. Freudenberger died in France, but his body was returned to the States and he was buried at Oak Grove Cemetery in Medford, Massachusetts, where he had family. Freudenberger's great-niece Wendy Howell confirmed that her family was from Medford.

It was a dark and starless night on November 2, 1918. Thick fog blanketed the waters of Vineyard Sound. November was a quiet month on Vineyard waters, and the captain of the tugboat *Covington* never expected to encounter another vessel as he steamed north, around West Chop, heading into Nantucket Sound.

The *Port Hunter*, a British supply ship, was steaming south through Vineyard Sound, heading to New York to join a convoy of ships crossing the Atlantic together under armed escort to avoid German U-boats. The *Port Hunter* was bound for Europe, loaded with supplies for soldiers fighting in the waning days of the First World War. It was deep in the darkest time of night.

The 5,500-ton *Port Hunter* was filled with military supplies and equipment for the war effort. Leather jerkins (jackets), hundreds of pairs of long woolen underwear, cozy wool socks, dozens of olive drab shirts and pants, and wool puttees (a covering of the lower leg from knee to ankle, like today's gaiters) made up some of the supplies for the troops, along with soap made from wool. The random list of supplies also included dozens and dozens of boxes

The *Port Hunter*, laden with war munitions and supplies for soldiers fighting, steamed through Vineyard Sound in early November 1918. *Stan Lair collection, courtesy of Chris Baer.*

The *Port Hunter* sank on Hedge Fence shoal. Locals looted the supply ship, hoarding army jackets and trench candles. *Stan Lair collection, courtesy of Chris Baer.*

of trench candles, steel rails, and eight hundred sets of railroad car wheels. Railroad engines, motorcycles, and steel billets (metal structures to house soldiers) were aboard. The *Port Hunter* carefully maneuvered its load of munitions and supplies around East Chop as it slowly steamed through the fog off Martha's Vineyard in the middle of the night.

At first, the captains of the two vessels were unaware of each other, yet the ships were on a collision course through the fog. Once they spotted each other in the gloaming, the captains of the *Covington* and the *Port Hunter* assumed the other would turn aside. Neither did. The *Covington* rammed the bow of the supply ship with such force that the *Port Hunter* stopped in place and immediately began to sink. The tugboat was undamaged.

The saving grace of the collision was that when the *Port Hunter* began to sink, the captain was able to maneuver the ship over Hedge Fence shoal, a shallow body of water in the Sound, a mile and a half off East Chop. The ship was disabled but sank only a few feet below the surface, resting on the ledge of Hedge Fence. The fifty-three sailors on board were never in danger; they were soon rescued, and locals provided food, clothing, shelter, and smokes. Life went on.

News of the sinking of the *Port Hunter* was described in the local press, but with no injuries or deaths, the story was not page-one material. No mention of any salvage operation or scavenging efforts made the newspaper.

What the *Gazette* chose to feature that week was news of the Armistice, which was big news. "The Gazette of November 7, 1918, gleefully noted the end of the war was in sight: 'Here in Edgartown the people are cheering, the church bells are ringing, the whistles are tooting, the dogs are barking, the autos are honking and verily it looks as if the old town might turn itself inside out.'"[4]

While celebrating the Armistice, wily Islanders set to work salvaging what they could of the military supplies aboard the submerged *Port Hunter*. In no time, Vineyarders paddled out to the sunken ship and absconded with whatever looked useful. They gathered up army jackets that could be sold. They took long underwear and wool socks.

The removal of military supplies continued through the fall and into the winter of 1919. By then, the War Department had realized army supplies were being stolen. The thievery had to stop. The army enlisted a New

This parade down Main Street, Vineyard Haven, in 1920 was typical of the celebration at the end of World War I. *Stan Lair collection, courtesy of Chris Baer.*

Bedford man, Barney Zeitz, to put a guard on the sunken ship to prevent more looting. Soon, however, the vessel sank below the surface, and the scavenging stopped. (Zeitz was the great-uncle of renowned stained-glass artist Barney Zeitz of Vineyard Haven.)

By the time the War Department realized devious activity was underway, Vineyarders were wearing long woolen underwear, deemed rather scratchy, and lighting stolen trench candles at parties. Creative Vineyarders sewed puttees into quilts, which proved warm in the chilly winter months. The leather jerkins or jackets were most popular; once washed at the local laundry to eliminate the salt water, they were hung out to dry on clotheslines around the Island.

Throughout the 1920s, the *Port Hunter* was mired on Hedge Fence shoal and in court cases determining what to do with the sunken hull. It was not until 1934 that a court ruled the *Port Hunter* was the property of William Fitzgerald, who had purchased the wreck in 1920 from the insurance company. A sometime partner of Fitzgerald named Smith had placed a buoy over the wreck and began his own salvaging operation. Fitzgerald took him to court, where the judge ruled there was no law on the admiralty books that allowed someone to place a buoy over a wreck, then claim it as his own.

In 2020...

In a nod to history, two new restaurants opened on opposite sides of Main Street in Edgartown. Although service was curtailed during the pandemic, the Port Hunter (2012) and the Covington (2016) offer upscale meals to hungry tourists and beverages to thirsty crowds who meander down the main street of the county seat.

2
PANDEMIC

The sinking of the *Port Hunter* excited scavengers across Martha's Vineyard. The Armistice, signed at the Palace of Versailles on November 11, dominated national news. A third story gained traction as word of a pandemic spread across the country.

The so-called Spanish flu was first reported in the United States at a Kansas military camp in March 1918 and spread across the country. Worldwide, 500 million people were infected, one-third of the earth's population. Some 50 million people died from the virus. In the United States, more than 675,000 Americans died during the 1918–19 influenza virus. (In comparison, by February 2022, more than 900,000 Americans had succumbed to the coronavirus COVID-19, with its Delta and Omicron variants. That number soon surpassed 1 million deaths.)

In 1920, the world population was 2 billion; 50 million died, equaling 2.5 percent.

In 2020, the world population was 8 billion; 6 million died worldwide, approximately .075 percent.

The population of the United States in 1920 was 106,020,000; 675,000 died (or .6 percent). The population of the United States in 2020 was 332,915,073; 1,000,000 died (or .3 percent). By the end of January 2023, 1,110,000 people had succumbed to COVID-19 and its variants in the United States; that is still about .33%.

Mary Cleveland Luce of West Tisbury, age sixty, was the first person on Martha's Vineyard to contract the influenza virus. She died of the infection in May 1918, shortly after getting sick. Her son-in-law Walter Vincent also died from the flu. The official death toll attributed to the disease on the Vineyard was only twelve, but more than likely an additional thirty or forty people on Island succumbed to the flu or related conditions and complications, primarily pneumonia.

There was no vaccine for the flu in 1918. People were advised to socially distance, to isolate or quarantine if infected, and many residents wore masks. Public schools on the Vineyard were closed for nearly three months; many students and staff were infected. Islanders understood that reducing social interaction could limit the spread of the flu.

Headlines in the *Boston Globe* in September 1918 read: "Influenza Adds 109 to Death List in Day." The story began, "Official order issued closing theatres and forbidding public gathering in Boston." Social distancing was recognized as a means of protection against catching the flu.

In September 1918, a second, deadlier strain of the virus that we know as H1N1 savaged the population across the state. Symptoms included a sore throat and headache, followed by the rapid onset of fever. Pneumonia soon followed, often leading to death.

Captain Walter Rheno of Vineyard Haven joined the Escadrille Lafayette fighter squadron in France and succumbed to the flu overseas. *Courtesy of the Martha's Vineyard Museum.*

"Early on Saturday morning, Sept. 21, 1918, the silent reaper entered the home of Mr. and Mrs. Jesse Smalley of Vineyard Haven and Gay Head, and claimed their son, Rodney Herbert, as the victim of pneumonia."[5] Smalley was only twenty years old; he was an apprentice mason and fisherman. Rodney was the youngest of three boys and "the pet of his home circle." A week before his death, Rodney Smalley had taken the first step to enlist in the army, as had so many of his fellow Wampanoag. He would have been the twenty-fourth Gay Head man to enlist.

Smalley was an active member of the Bradley Memorial Baptist Church in Oak Bluffs. Reverend Oscar Denniston performed his funeral ceremony, attended by many friends and family. Elsie Diamond and Netta Vanderhoop participated in the funeral service. Smalley was buried in the Gay Head cemetery on Rose Meadow.

This tragedy was followed shortly by the death of Clara (Rheno) Tennis, "one of the Vineyard's most attractive young women," according to the *Vineyard Gazette* of September 26, 1918. Tennis, a twenty-five-year-old nurse from Vineyard Haven, "was stricken with the Spanish influenza, developing pneumonia," on her honeymoon. Her brother Walter Rheno, an aviator with the Foreign Legion, also caught the strain and died overseas. Tennis was buried in the family plot in the Oak Grove Cemetery in Oak Bluffs.

A note on the name *Spanish flu*: Spain was neutral during the First World War. There was no censorship in Spain, as in other countries that sought to curtail fear of a dread epidemic during the war. The Spanish press was uncensored, free to publish in-depth news reports of the pandemic sweeping across Europe. Newspaper readers learned about the epidemic and assumed it began in and was limited to Spain.

No one knows for sure exactly when and where the flu began: France, England, China, or the United States. The first case in the States was reported on March 11, 1918, at a military base in Kansas.

A jingle of the era, posted in the New York press, read,

Cover up each cough and sneeze,
If you don't, you'll spread disease.

Daniel Pierce, a street peddler in his mid-sixties, passed away on the Vineyard that autumn. Blinded as a child, Pierce sold trinkets and tchotchke to tourists who rode the Martha's Vineyard Railroad in the 1880s and '90s as the train chugged from Cottage City to Depot Station in Edgartown then on to South Beach in Katama. Pierce was said to be the last town crier who walked the streets of Edgartown, calling out the news of the day.

The *Vineyard Gazette* of December 12, 1918, offered healthy suggestions and information to convalescents of the flu. According to the Public Health Service, "Beware tuberculosis after influenza," warned the surgeon general. Early treatment is best. "Build up your strength with right living, good food and plenty of fresh air." Patients should take care of themselves to avoid reinfection. "Become a fresh air crank and enjoy life," admonished the *Gazette*.

By mid-December, nearly one million tuberculosis cases raged across the United States. The surgeon general warned people not to diagnose themselves but to seek medical advice if they had a cold that lingered or found that they were falling into decline; both were signs of possible TB. And be cautious of fraudulent cures, the surgeon general added. "Above all do not trust in the misleading statements or unscrupulous patent medicine fakers."

Three Edgartown men died of the flu on the same day, December 17, 1918. Wendall Ripley, age twenty-one, worked as an assistant purser on the *Uncatena* steamship. Albert Lambert, age thirty-six, was a "member of Nunnepeg Tribe of Red Men of Edgartown." And Gerald Pease, age thirty-four, was known to be "prominent in town, county and social affairs." News of the third death that same day in Edgartown "was received with universal sorrow, and…a pall of gloom fell over the whole community."

The next day, Frank Howard, age thirty-five, died, "well known by all in the community."

The Island was ravaged by the pandemic in the final month of 1918.

The *Gazette* reported that the deaths were all caused by fatal illnesses that followed influenza.

Freeman Smith, a deaf clay digger in Chilmark, died from the flu on New Year's Day 1919.

In the first six months of 1919, two more strains of the flu filtered across the country. These proved to be milder strains, with fewer deaths associated with them.

President Woodrow Wilson contracted, but survived, the influenza while working on negotiations that culminated in the Treaty of Versailles, which ended the First World War. The treaty was signed in the Hall of Mirrors in Versailles, outside Paris, on June 28, 1919.

One of the last people diagnosed with the H1H1 virus was Frank Eddy, age thirty-four. Eddy was manager of the telephone exchange, located at the current site of Rainy Day on Main Street, Vineyard Haven.

By the summer of 1919, the influenza pandemic had receded, not only on Martha's Vineyard but also across Massachusetts and around the world.

Over the last century, the effect of this dread influenza faded into the forgotten pages of history until COVID-19 took center stage early in 2020 and beyond.

Martha's Vineyard Magazine acknowledged the 1918 pandemic a century after it occurred, under the caption "Encyclopedia Vineyardia." The story began with the single word, *Influenza*, and described it as the "cause of the global pandemic in 1918 known as the Spanish flu, which killed at least nineteen people on the Island starting in September of that year." The piece mentioned the death of Rodney Smalley and the three Edgartown young men who died in mid-December.

"Edgartown has thus lost much of her young manhood, a series of sad events which it would be hard to find duplicated in her past history. It is hoped that the disease which has caused so much sorrow in so many homes is now about run out."[6] After printing the sorrowful news about three young Edgartown men dying on the same day, the *Gazette* noted that there were no more serious flu cases on Island to report.

In 2022...

A century after the pandemic of 1918, we acknowledge the dreadful effect of COVID-19 across the country. The virus spread fear and concern around the Island with dozens of cases. Only one death has been attributed to the disease on Martha's Vineyard: Albert Hutchinson, age seventy-eight, of Chilmark, died in February 2022.

3

PROHIBITION I

In the years before the Civil War, the Sons of Temperance proved a dominant force in Holmes Hole (now Vineyard Haven), restricting Island youth from gaining access to alcohol. The rowdies moved on to Edgartown, where the current law was laxer. Alcohol was supposed to be purchased only for medicinal purposes, but the young men of the 1850s had more than health on their minds.

Public drunkenness led to arrest in the nineteenth century, as it does today. Records from the Edgartown jail indicate Black and Native American citizens were more often jailed for alcohol abuse than white people; however, that was due to racial prejudice, not because they drank more. Prejudice across Martha's Vineyard in the nineteenth century was an issue, as it has been for decades. Once arrested, the drunken soul was incarcerated for the night yet often incurred repeat offenses.

In the early twentieth century, the temperance movement attracted more adherents. The theory was that by eliminating alcohol, poverty would be reduced, family life would improve, and social ills would evaporate, as if by magic.

Two Constitutional amendments, the Eighteenth in 1920 and the Twenty-First in 1933, bookend the 1920s.

The Eighteenth Amendment was ratified by three-fourths of the states on January 16, 1919, two months after the end of the First World War. It became the law of the land a year later.

This amendment prohibited the production, transportation, and sale of intoxicating liquor. The accompanying Volstead Act imposed the same requirements for beer and wine. Interestingly, there was no penalty for the actual consumption of alcohol. It was only illegal to make, move, or sell it. Drink as much as you could get your hands on; just don't brew it, transport it, or sell it.

The Constitutional amendment to prohibit the manufacture, distribution, and sale of liquor ignited a series of unintended consequences that spread through the country. Sparks from the prohibition on the sale of alcohol incinerated the Roaring Twenties. Eventually, the Eighteenth Amendment was doused and repealed by the Twenty-First Amendment in 1933.

Arthur Railton, the erstwhile editor of the Dukes County Historical Society's *Intelligencer* (now the Martha's Vineyard Museum's *MV Quarterly*), railed, "Islanders had never been enthusiastic Prohibitionists." In his lengthy account of Vineyard history, "How We Got to Where We Are," Railton observed, "The Island, its miles of remote beaches easily accessible to rum-running boats, discovered a new way to make money, illegal though it was."[7]

The centennial of the Eighteenth Amendment occurred in 2020, and Geoff Currier of the *MV Times* was ready with a review. "This year [2020] marks the 100th anniversary of the 18th Amendment, a constitutional ban on the production and sale of alcoholic beverages that can be seen as the very definition of unintended consequences. Rather than eliminating liquor, this act did more to instill a culture of drinking in a thirsty nation than 100,000 happy hours."[8]

Currier delighted in describing details of rumrunning operations off the shores of Martha's Vineyard. "In addition to the fishing boats, many Vineyarders who had a fast boat, and a heightened sense of adventure would wait for a moonless night and venture out to the supply ships themselves." The spirit of adventure and danger was very real between the shoreline and the Rum Row supply ships, legally a dozen miles out to sea. That watery slice of ocean was patrolled by the Coast Guard, eager to spot, chase, and catch small fishing boats and naïve Vineyarders, trapped between the law and a probable financial reward.

For more than a decade, Martha's Vineyard became a haven for those who brewed, shipped, and sold alcohol. Many tales from those days were never told because, like the Underground Railroad, talking, writing, or reporting on illegal activities exposed the reporter to criminal inquisition and potential liability: you were complicit in the crime if you did nothing to stop it.

That said, tales from the Prohibition era have slithered under the door into public view to stand on their own. Many more events went unrecorded when the participants sank to their watery graves.

The principal definition of someone who transported liquor during the 1920s was a rumrunner. The word *hooch* entered the vocabulary as a name for illicit alcohol. Hooch refers to a Native American tribe in Alaska that distilled alcohol. Arctic whaleman George Fred Tilton brought it back with him on one of his whaling ventures.

Another Island character, Craig Kingsbury (1913–2002), earned a reputation in various venues, claiming to be the first to introduce skunks to Martha's Vineyard and serving as a salty language tutor to Robert Shaw in *Jaws*. Kingsbury eagerly offered his recollections of Prohibition, although he was only six when the Eighteenth Amendment was ratified. "There was no problem getting a drink during Prohibition," he told the museum's Arthur Railton.[9]

During the 1920s, the Coast Guard was charged with preventing the transfer of alcohol by boat. This proved virtually impossible. The culprits were often fishermen, engaged in rumrunning to supplement their day jobs. Fishermen are not criminals at heart. Fishermen would offer food to the crew aboard the supply ship; they opted not to share what they were given in exchange for the food.

The initial assignment for the Coast Guard was to patrol ocean waters within three miles of the coastline. In 1923, the limit was extended to twelve miles, which made the job of patrolling the shores far more challenging for the Coast Guard to enforce.

The twelve-mile limit was established to keep supply ships farther offshore. It did. Supply ships, also known as "mother ships," respected the twelve-mile limit because that was legal. Transportation of alcohol from Scotland and the West Indies or homemade hooch were also legal, provided it was at least a dozen miles offshore. Often rumrunners waited to meet their mother ships on Georges Bank, a popular fishing site.

Danger and arrest accompanied rumrunning. The captain and crew of small vessels purchased liquor from the mother ship, transported it back to shore, unloaded it in the dark of night, and sold it. All that was illegal. Many of those so-called fishermen in reality were rumrunners, racing back to the Island or the mainland with their illegal hooch. They were essentially criminals and subject to capture and arrest by the Coast Guard. It was not a safe or easy way to make a buck.

Fishermen worked the waters by day then ran rum at night. Earning two incomes made for a profitable, if dangerous, lifestyle. *Courtesy of the Bradford Tavern.*

Commercial fishermen proved successful rumrunners. They had to be out in the ocean anyway. They knew the waters around Martha's Vineyard and often could outsmart or outrun the Coast Guard. Many Vineyarders were fishing for their livelihood. When the opportunity afforded itself, Island fishermen were enticed by the substantial financial reward to provide alcohol to thirsty Vineyarders. Fishermen caught cod or flounder by day, then transported rum or whiskey by night, making a tidy profit from two careers on ocean waters.

"They [the fishermen] were carrying two separate cargoes: one, very visible, was the layers of fresh fish bedded down in chopped ice; the other, at the bottom of the fish hold, hidden from view, was the real cash-crop, liquor."[10] Canvas covered the bottles of liquor, protected with another layer of ice.

Initially, bottles were stored in wooden boxes. Later, canvas sacks proved more functional to hoist bottles of booze aboard and store in a small fishing vessel, then unloaded into the back of a bootlegger's truck late at night. It was a full-time job, two careers working in tandem. The era of Prohibition offered the hint of danger as well as reward, unplanned results of the Eighteenth Amendment.

An early report on rumrunning appeared in the *Vineyard Gazette*, eighteen months after Prohibition began. The headline mentioned mysterious whistles offshore and strange craft making trips to the mainland. "According to stories of fishermen and yachtsmen, 'rum-runners' are plying a regular trade between the Vineyard and the mainland." Locals shared the name of the vessel, which had been spotted often "under suspicious circumstances."[11]

The report relates, "Summer residents on the sound side of the island tell of hearing whistles coming in irregular sequence after dark, as if signaling were going on. Old timers cannot remember anything of this nature before, and they infer that the signaling has to do with the moonshine business." Firsthand accounts stated, "If the nocturnal tootings are correctly designated, it would seem that something larger than catboats or motor craft must trade."

Dorothy Scoville explained how simple the rumrunning business was: "Small, fast boats played a cat and mouse game with the slower Coast Guard patrol boats. They loaded rum from an off shore supply ship and ran it in to some secluded shore where it was picked up by trucks or passenger cars with extra heavy springs that disguised the weight of the load."[12]

Rumrunning was publicly acknowledged. Early on, there was no mention of Coast Guard interference. The illicit activity of rumrunning was rampant around the Island and up and down the East Coast.

On August 10, 1921, the *New Bedford Evening Standard* sent a reporter disguised as a fisherman to investigate a rumrunner off Noman's Land, the small island southeast of Martha's Vineyard. Reporter Earle Wilson, "posing as a thirsty customer," enticed the skipper of a fishing boat to take him out to the *Arethusa*, a mother ship on Rum Row. Wilson's story, published in the *Evening Standard*, broke the news of the illegal activity aboard ship, "dispensing refreshment in a truly hospitable manner to all drought-ridden individuals who can sail, row or swim out to the trim-looking fisherman." The schooner *Arethusa* flew a British flag, anchored more than twenty miles offshore, and the skipper was Bill McCoy of New London, Connecticut.[13]

Notorious rumrunner Bill McCoy boasted that he provided illegal alcohol to the south shore and Islands during Prohibition. *Courtesy of drinkingcup.net.*

The *Standard* article continues: "Captain Bill McCoy, who was one of the first group of skippers to go into the business of smuggling liquor—he had never been on the wrong side of the law before and took pride in having his cargo known as 'the real McCoy.'" McCoy famously claimed that he never watered down his liquor.

McCoy claimed the *Arethusa* was the first rumrunner to ply its trade off the Massachusetts coast. He valued his privacy. For a while, he lived in Gay Head among the Wampanoag because the Natives neither asked questions nor talked to strangers. They respected McCoy's privacy and had no reason to say anything to the Coast Guard.

Brashly, McCoy boasted to reporter/fisherman Earle Wilson that "we manage to supply Block Island, Martha's Vineyard, New Bedford and Fall River with what the residents of those places seem to want the most." That was the fodder Wilson sought.

The lead story in the *New Bedford Evening Standard* that day dissuaded the crew of the *Arethusa* from unloading some 140 cases of liquor on the Vineyard. Within two days of the front-page story, the *Arethusa* was no longer in the area. Customers were disappointed, the Coast Guard was temporarily relieved, and new means and methods of transport were devised.

In Geoff Currier's perspective on Prohibition, he cited McCoy's crew in their efforts at subterfuge: "To avoid recognition when their reprehensible past was behind them, they all grew beards of untamed luxuriance, and since the schooner had been out for a long time and fresh water was scarce, they rarely washed. They looked like Airedales and smelled like camels."[14]

He added, "Through the lens of time, rumrunning can take on a sanitized patina, appearing to be a harmless cat and mouse game between the Coast Guard and daredevil mariners. But make no mistake, it often led to dire consequences."

"If we train our eyes and hearts to search for the good and beautiful around us, we can always find them, for there are rainbows to be seen in the spray during the wildest gales, if we but look for them." Annie Wood (1876–1930) penned these words in the preface of her posthumous memoir *Noman's Land: Isle of Romance*. This was not a book about Prohibition but about the beauty of the isolated island three miles off Martha's Vineyard.[15]

Noman's Land is 860 acres of glacial drift, rocks, boulders, and erratic that glaciers pushed across the land thousands of years ago. The island has a rugged, raw coastline, five miles around. Its south shore is constantly battered by the wind and waves of the Atlantic. (During World War II, and continuing to 1996, Noman's was used for bombing practice by the U.S. Navy. Today it is off-limits to visitors due to the danger of unexploded bombs.)

Annie Wood's book describes a specific rumrunning event: "The wrecking of the *Flit*, a steam yacht about one hundred feet long, on the shore at Noman's Land in 1923, was one of the strangest incidents that ever took place on the island."[16] She explained, "It was rumored that she was used as a supply, or mother ship, for several small boats engaged in rum running." The *Flit* met foreign vessels out at sea to transfer liquor aboard, and "on her return, she was met within a few miles of Noman's Land by several small boats to which the load was transferred."

"One of the most mysterious instances of rumrunner deaths in the whole Prohibition era concerns the matter of the former pogy steamer John Dwight," wrote Everett Allen, author of *Black Ships*. "On the morning of April 6, 1923, the *John Dwight* was spotted midway in Vineyard Sound, between Gay Head and Cuttyhunk. Heavy fog was rolling in. The Cuttyhunk Coast Guard sighted the ship and presumed she was in distress; they set out to investigate."

The saga unfolded, in slow motion, from various perspectives. "A small cloud of steam was coming from the starboard side, and the stern of the *Dwight* was slowly settling." The *John Dwight* sank silently into the Sound.[17]

When they encountered bottles of Frontenac ale, brewed in Canada, the Gay Head Coast Guard crew knew they had reached the site of a rumrunning venture gone awry. At the time of discovery, there was no evidence of crew or any other debris from the *John Dwight.*

The next day, April 7, the bodies of seven crew members in life jackets were found floating in the Sound. An eighth man, his head bashed in, lay in a lifeboat on the Menemsha shore. That man was identified as Harry King, son of one of two men listed as captains of the *John Dwight.* Vineyard Haven sheriff Walter Renear reported that "nearly all the bodies picked up in the sound bore evidence of a wicked, free-for-all fight. There was [*sic*] lacerations and bruises about their faces that came from contact with some solid, blunt instrument."[18]

The *John Dwight,* built in 1896, had been a lighter, rigged to lift heavy cargo. The *Dwight* was used to hoist sunken coal barges for the navy. More recently, the *Dwight* had been outfitted in Newport for the rumrunning trade. John King was listed as one captain; Malcolm Carmichael was the second, likely the navigator.

The destroyer *Dorchester* passed the site shortly after the sinking. The crew spotted a small boat with three men rowing urgently toward Naushon Island. Later, the dory and two name-boards from the *John Dwight* were found on Naushon, but no sign of the missing captains.

The *John Dwight* was assumed to be a rumrunner from a mother ship. It sank (or was intentionally sunk) on April 6, 1923. The story made the *New York Times.* The *Gazette* reported on April 12 that "bodies of her crew were found floating amongst bottles of bootleg ale in Vineyard Sound." Although the men wore life jackets, their deaths were attributed to drowning. The mystery continued.

A later account postulated, "The men at the Gay Head Lifeboat Station heard sounds of whistles and bells coming across the water through the fog and prepared to launch their boats for the rescue of the steamer in Vineyard Sound. Then they saw the ship roll, explode, and sink. The next day they found the bodies of the crew members in life jackets floating nearby among bottles of illegal ale."

Crew from another steamer, the *Flit,* apparently escaped when their vessel grounded on Noman's Land.

"One popular theory is that the captains and perhaps some of the crew scuttled the steamer and murdered its crew in order to swindle them out of the bootlegging venture." The *Gazette* added helpfully: "Many cases of liquor have been picked up in the Sound, including ale and Scotch whiskey."[19]

Later, the two captains surfaced in Havana but refused to share their account of the *Dwight.*

"Two principal theories—piracy and mutiny—emerged and persist to this day." It was known that a large sum of money was aboard the *John Dwight*, but whether it was payment for liquor or some other scheme was unknown. None of the rumored stash was ever discovered.[20]

New Bedford Standard Times reporter Earle Wilson determined the sinking of the *Dwight* was a case of piracy. "The purpose of the *Dwight*'s trip could not have been secret. It must have been known to many men to whom $100,000 would be a sufficient sum to justify anything, even the cold-blooded murder of fifteen men."

Diver David Curney explored the *Dwight* as he had the *Port Hunter*. He found no more alcohol or bodies aboard the *Dwight* but was unable to do more than a cursory dive as the waters were chilly and the current rapid.

Chris Baer summarized the mystery of the *John Dwight*: "Another notable sea battle went mostly unrecorded in 1923 except for the eight corpses found floating in Vineyard Sound off the Chilmark shore, Cedar Tree Neck, and Menemsha—the result of what was evidently a violent massacre of the crew of the rumrunner *John Dwight* off Cuttyhunk by criminals unknown."[21]

Two great-grandchildren of Captain John King surfaced in 2015. They shared frustration at the mystery that hovered over their great-grandfather's exploits. Their grandmother, King's daughter and sister to crew member Harry King, sought information but had found nothing except for what had already been in the press.

Another piece of the puzzle surfaced in Annie Wood's book on Noman's. It was postulated that the crew of the *Flit* engaged the *John Dwight* in a bitter naval encounter, a rumrunning deal gone bad. The crew of the *John Dwight* were killed, except for the men who rowed ashore. The crew of the *Flit* then opened the sea valves of the *John Dwight* so it sank in Vineyard Sound. "The *Flit* was run over to Noman's Land, driven up onto the beach and abandoned. It is not known whether any of them [*Flit* crew] were killed or injured."[22]

It seems coincidental that the grounding of the *Flit* on Noman's occurred at the same time as the sinking of the *John Dwight*, and clearly both were linked to rumrunning. However, no more information has surfaced to shed accurate information on what occurred on that foggy April morn a century ago.

No one ever returned to Noman's to claim the *Flit*; it was stripped of its fine furnishings. Coast Guardsmen sought to track down the crew without success. The story feels incomplete, lacking more sordid details. As in many tales of rumrunning, it's unlikely anyone who knew what happened ever wanted to share the details.

In 1920...
Henry Beetle Hough and Betty Bowie were married. Hough's father, New Bedford newspaperman George Hough, purchased the *Vineyard Gazette* for $5,000 as a wedding present for them.

4

SUFFRAGE

The primary of September 1920 was the first election after passage of the Nineteenth Amendment. On the Vineyard, the election marked nothing new in the results: "The Democratic vote was slim as usual."[23] Across the Island, a total of thirteen votes were cast for Democrats. In the 1920s, Martha's Vineyard was a Republican stronghold; it continued that way throughout the decade.

Nevertheless, "A large proportion of the women registered in the different towns went to the polls and voted. In West Tisbury the voters numbered 36 men and 24 women. Fully half the women registered in Vineyard Haven were checked at the polls. The vote of the women was fairly heavy everywhere."[24]

In the pivotal presidential election that November, the first after World War I, 1,168 voters went to the polls on Martha's Vineyard. That was a significant increase over the election of 1916, when only 787 men turned out to vote, before the country entered the war. The obviously higher number of voters can and should be attributed to passage of the Nineteenth Amendment to the Constitution: women now had the right to vote. And they used it.

The higher number of voters on the Vineyard was directly related to passage of the amendment. This parallels the historic election of 1868. The Fourteenth Amendment assured Black men of their citizenship and with that the right to vote. In the election of 1868, Republican Ulysses S. Grant defeated Democrat Horatio Seymour, former governor of New York. Seymour had opposed President Lincoln's administration during the Civil War and was an advocate of President Andrew Johnson. More than half a million recently registered Black men overwhelmingly turned out for General Grant.

QUALIFIED WOMEN VOTERS

In the Town of Tisbury, Mass.

Certified to February 10 '31.

Wm. S. Swift Town Clerk

Many women were registered to vote in this 1931 register. Great excitement was generated by passage of the Nineteenth Amendment. *Courtesy of the Martha's Vineyard Museum.*

This ballot box served local voters. It was stored in the police department, the former town hall. *Photo by Oak Bluffs Police Department.*

"'Island Happy,' was the election headline in 1920, appearing over a cut of the enigmatic face of Calvin Coolidge, elected vice president on the ticket with Harding."[25] Results of the 1920 election indicated that Dukes County recorded 1,013 votes for Republican Warren Harding for president. It helped to have Massachusetts governor Calvin Coolidge on the ticket as vice president.

Of the Island electorate, 86 percent favored the Harding-Coolidge presidential ticket over Democrat James Cox, who ran with Franklin Roosevelt, assistant secretary of the navy, for vice president. (Keep an eye on that defeated vice-presidential candidate. We'll hear from him at the end of the decade.) Socialist Eugene Debs also ran for president.

In this first year of female suffrage, forty-nine-year-old Almah Pease Jernegan of Edgartown was the first woman in town to cast her vote for the president of the United States. In West Tisbury, Emma Terry was the first woman to cast a ballot. In Chilmark, it was Florence Blackwell Mayhew.

In early August 1921, Vice President Calvin Coolidge, Grace Coolidge, and their two sons visited the Vineyard for several days, staying at Mohu, the private estate of William and Mary Butler on Lamberts Cove Road, and later the property of *Washington Post* publisher Katharine Graham. The fifty-acre site on the Vineyard's north shore, facing the Elizabeth Islands across Vineyard Sound, includes more than eight hundred feet of private beach and shoreline along James Pond.

At the vice president's request, no public reception was planned. The Coolidge party sped across Vineyard Sound in the Butlers' private yacht *Akoar* and later enjoyed "motor trips about the island, when he called on many old friends."[26]

One old friend whom Coolidge visited was Edwin D. Vanderhoop, who served a term in the state legislature in 1888, the only Native American

COOLIDGE VISITS VINEYARD

Vice-President Guest of Mr. and Mrs. William M. Butler.

Vice President and Mrs. Coolidge and their two sons, have been the guests of Mr. and Mrs. William M. Butler at Mohu, their Lambert's Cove estate, for several days. They letf Tuesday. Others in the party at Mohu included Mr. and Mrs. Frank Stearns of Boston, and a member of the secret service.

At his own urgent request there was no public reception of this distinguished guest. His presence on the island was not generally known until he was about to leave. His time was spent on the Butler speed Yacht, Akoar, which brought him over from Woods Hole, in motor trips about the island, when he called on many old friends, and in enjoying the delights of beautiful Mohu. He attended the concert held in Edgartown for the benefit of the Legion and of the Cottage Hospital, at which Mrs. Morgan Butler sang.

(Continued on Page 5)

Vice President Calvin Coolidge visited Martha's Vineyard in 1921, accompanied by a single Secret Service agent. *Courtesy of the* Vineyard Gazette.

in Massachusetts ever to earn that honor. Vanderhoop acknowledged the Coolidge visit with a letter to the editor, writing, in part: "I was so surprised when I came to the door to see before me The [*sic*] Vice President of the Great United States that I was speechless, to express my pleasure and appreciation by words for the presence of my distinguished guests at my humble home for the inquiry of my health."

Coolidge also paid his respects to another former state representative, Ulysses E. Mayhew. Before serving in the state legislature, Mayhew (1848–1939) had been a whaleman aboard a vessel sunk by the Confederate raider *Alabama* during the Civil War. He worked for P.T. Barnum's circus and served as a vice president in the early years of the Dukes County Historical Society.

Coolidge and Mayhew first met in the General Court in 1907. Mayhew's daughter, Emma Terry, was the first woman to cast a ballot in West Tisbury in the 1920 election,

Also included in the busy week was a concert in Edgartown to benefit the Legion and the Cottage Hospital.

Two years later, Coolidge became president on the death of Warren Harding in 1923.

In the 1924 election, President Coolidge and his running mate Charles Dawes defeated John Davis and Charles Bryan. Robert La Follette ran as a Progressive candidate. Coolidge won 62 percent of the votes in Massachusetts. On the Vineyard, a total of 1,360 Vineyard voters cast their ballots, with 86 percent supporting Republican Calvin Coolidge.

In 2020...

Republican state legislatures sought to make it more difficult for minority and young voters to cast their ballots: "Forty-three states, including Georgia, have together introduced over 250 bills to restrict voting access after the 2020 election as of Friday, according to the Brennan Center for Justice. The measures limit mail-in voting, impose stricter voter identification requirements, purge voter rolls, and make voter registration more difficult, according to the Center."[27]

5

FASHION

In the 1920s, women who felt emboldened to act unconventionally were called flappers.

This was an era of empowerment for young women. Freedom-loving females united in a spirit of camaraderie, rebelling against the restraints of an earlier era. And the older, staid populace was horrified by their dramatically independent lifestyle.

The word *flapper* dates back centuries, but in the early 1900s, it referred to young women, teenagers whose hair was not put up, so it flapped on their backs. A flapper could be a spritely young woman, a teenage girl swinging or flapping her arms. A flapper might be an acrobatic performer or a dancer who flapped like a bird, dancing the Charleston. Flappers could be mischievous, flirtatious, intent on living a lively lifestyle from dancing and partying to drinking and smoking. Fashion meant looseness, with coats unbuttoned, hair bobbed, flapping in the breeze as the woman walked briskly to her next rendezvous.

Independent, perhaps immature, the word *flapper* assumed different definitions and insinuations. Freedom-loving, inspired, and inspirational characterized these highly motivated, unconventional young women. Flappers ruled.

In fashion, from 1910 to 1920, dresses were full and often full-length. In the 1920s, dresses were slim, with lower necklines, often sleeveless, with drop waists, ruffles on the skirts, and hemlines just below the knee to mid-calf. Flappers wore short hair (bobbed) and short skirts (knee-length), frowned on as being unfeminine by reserved Victorians.

Gibson girls were flappers, typical of the 1920s, caring more about their own wants and wishes than trying to please a man. They were athletic, refined, and calm examples of the New Woman, apolitical but appreciative of the right to vote. Flappers wore lots of makeup, exhibited disdain for conventional behavior and enjoyed listening to jazz, smoking, and drinking, often in public. These new women were not subservient to men; they lived their own lives as they wanted. Flappers treated sex as a casual encounter yet were curious about birth control.

The primary element of a flapper lifestyle was to do as she pleased. Living unconventionally was the convention of flappers in the 1920s.

National experiences influenced this newfound independence among young women, the flappers of the Roaring Twenties. From economic opportunity to political power to social strength and cultural custom, young women expressed their freedom from constraints and regulations across the board. Independent women seized the spotlight with their capacity to change the mores of American life.

Martha's Vineyard was not immune to this national awakening.

The First World War expanded the workforce with the manufacture of munitions. As men were conscripted, factories needed more workers. Immigration was curtailed, and women were employed by the war machine. Large companies paid a higher wage than small businesses, so women who went to work in factories came home with more money. On the Vineyard, although there were no factories, there were jobs available in town offices and small businesses when the men went off to war.

"I think mom and her girlfriends were more like Flappettes," said Joan Boyken, whose mother, Maude Littlefield, grew up on Martha's Vineyard in the 1920s. "When the 1920s began mom was eleven; she left the Island when she was eighteen or nineteen because there wasn't any work there." Maude Littlefield and her friend relocated to Newark, New Jersey, to work. "I do know that my mom was fun loving, she smoked and drank and was a, to put it in a 1950s word, a kook. I am proud to take after her."[28]

More money in a woman's pocket meant more money to spend.

The Nineteenth Amendment to the Constitution finally gave women the right to vote. That sense of independence proved an asset for women to voice their political judgment. The power of the ballot cannot be underestimated; it offered a sense of independence.

Left: Teenager Maude Littlefield lived in Oak Bluffs until she graduated from high school. She always loved the Vineyard and is buried in town. *Courtesy of Joan Boyken.*

Right: "My mother was more of a Flapperette," said her daughter. Maude smoked on occasion and partied with the best of them. *Courtesy of Joan Boyken.*

Advances in contraception offered another sense of freedom for the women of the 1920s. No longer constrained by luck or chance, women valued knowledge of the reproductive system and ability to control their bodies. The means and methods of birth control, from the sponge to the diaphragm, were shared among young women. Flappers appreciated the options of birth control in planning and living their lives.

Mass production of automobiles also affected flappers.

In 1908, the Ford Motor Company introduced the Model T, an efficient vehicle offered at a reasonable price. By mass-producing the Model T on an assembly line, Ford made affordable cars available for young women. The company flourished in the 1920s; two-thirds of the automobile market consisted of Ford products, the majority being the ubiquitous Model T. On the Vineyard, more than half of all automobiles were Fords, according to a 1923 survey. And women were driving many of them.

The automobile offered unlimited opportunity for travel, freedom, and independence. Young women were enthralled at the opportunity to live their own lives, especially behind the wheel.

When the Eighteenth Amendment to the Constitution was passed, Prohibition ushered in an era of illegality that contributed to the flapper movement. Rumrunning, bathtub gin, speakeasies, and fast living inspired independence, bordering on criminality. Think Bonnie and Clyde. While we don't have evidence of young women running rum from mother ships along Rum Row to Martha's Vineyard, it was not illegal to drink the prohibited potion, and what woman would turn down a drink?

Multiple experiences contributed to the rise of flappers. Once a young woman recognized the opportunities afforded by higher wages, the right to vote, birth control, a Tin Lizzie, and an illicit drink, that opened the door to smoking in public, fast dancing, cutting-edge attire with a cultural appreciation for jazz, tuning in to the radio, and enjoying silent movies.

Today, we take these cultural customs for granted. However, in the Roaring Twenties, women who had been restrained by Victorian sensibilities over the generations eagerly took advantage of the opportunity to flex their muscles, shake their shoulders, swing their arms, and assume a new identity. The Roaring Twenties opened the door for young women, and it has never closed behind them.

In her photo album, Maude Littlefield wrote, "if this car could talk." *Courtesy of Joan Boyken.*

6
MUSIC

In the early years of the twentieth century, the Vineyard Haven Band would often play three concerts a day over the three days the Agricultural Fair was underway at the Grange Hall in West Tisbury. The band played summer concerts on Sunday evenings, alternating between Vineyard Haven and Oak Bluffs, as it does today.

In 1919, the band changed its name from the Vineyard Haven Brass Band to simply the Vineyard Haven Band. However, women and woodwinds were still denied participation in band programs. Yet the band played on.

Composer Harry Burleigh (1866–1949) "was a baritone, a classical composer, an arranger and a soloist. His musical legend lives on in his collection of Negro spirituals entitled *Jubilee Songs of the United States of America*."[29] Burleigh was a New Yorker but frequently vacationed on the Vineyard, regularly staying at Shearer Cottage.

Dorothy West knew Harry Burleigh, "the composer, who left a priceless legacy in his long research of Negro spirituals—those shouts of grace and suffering and redemption that might have perished forever if he had not given his gifts to preserving them—he was the first to bring back glad tidings of the Island's fair land to his New York friends, who had always thought of Massachusetts as a nice place to come from, but not to go to unless bound and gagged."[30]

Burleigh and his son traveled to Europe in 1925 and returned to spend the rest of the summer at Shearer Cottage as was his wont. He was a regular performer on the radio and occasionally sang at Union Chapel in Oak Bluffs. Two of his anthem arrangements were performed in 1928, as the *Gazette* reported: "Burleigh, one of the country's eminent composers, a noted baritone," joined the choir in "Were You There When They Crucified Him" and "Deep River." Harry Burleigh was a prominent, popular, and seasoned professional who valued his time in Oak Bluffs.

Another regular at Shearer Cottage was Lillian Evanti, the first professional Black opera singer. Evanti, a soprano, sang with Marian Anderson at the Belasco Theatre in her native Washington, D.C., in 1926. The Belasco was one of the few theaters in the District of Columbia where Black performers were invited to sing. The event was produced in conjunction with the football game between Howard University, Evanti's alma mater, and Lincoln University. During the Roosevelt administration, Evanti sang at the White House. And when she visited Martha's Vineyard, she stayed at Shearer Cottage.

The 1920s was built on postwar prosperity along with frenetic music (think the Charleston and the Foxtrot).

Jazz came into its own in the '20s. Everyone seemed to be into jazz. Soloists improvised on trumpets, trombones, and clarinets. "Each instrument had a defined role, but the music was improvised. Arrangements for swing focused on an intense rhythm with repeated riffs. Soloists would be featured, with the rhythm section providing the beat. Improvisation allowed the musicians an artistic freedom of self-expression."[31]

Jazz improv musicians ruled, with swing as the most popular, although waltz music was also in vogue. Swing appropriated the style of jazz in the 1930s, with big bands in dance halls or music from recordings or radio. "Freedom and abandon in the improvisational musical style offered a release and an escape from the anguish and suffering of the Great Depression."[32]

For decades, the hub of summer activity in Oak Bluffs was the Tivoli dance hall, which opened in 1907 and closed in 1964. It was located at the site of the current police department. Tivoli, spelled backward, reads: "I lov it."

The Tivoli dominated downtown Oak Bluffs with its imposing two-story structure, hosting a dance hall upstairs, with attractions below including a

Above: The Tivoli was a magnet, attracting partygoers and dancers from all over. *Courtesy of the Martha's Vineyard Museum.*

Right: Will Hardy was the consummate bandmaster, writing and conducting songs such as the "Oak Bluffs Galop" and "Tivoli Girl." *Courtesy of the Martha's Vineyard Museum.*

The dance floor of the Tivoli was rarely empty. Music from the Novelty Orchestra drifted up Circuit Avenue and along the shore. *Courtesy of the Martha's Vineyard Museum.*

shooting gallery and an ice cream parlor. "It was a magnet, attracting not only summer people, but year-round Islanders as well."[33]

Will Hardy brought his sextet from Worcester each summer and played at the Tivoli, songs he composed himself. For fifteen years, he and his Novelty Orchestra dominated the scene, often playing his tunes "Tivoli Girl" and the "Oak Bluffs Galop."

Accolades came from all over. "It was Will Hardy's sextet that created the magic of the Tivoli. You didn't have to dance to feel the Tivoli magic. Thousands were enthralled by the music as they strolled along Circuit Avenue."[34] Hardy, both composer and bandleader, played at the Tivoli until 1931.

In 1928, historian and musician Gale Huntington was intrigued when he heard that "Welcome [Tilton] wants to have a musical time."[35] When young Huntington met the older man, Tilton proved a major influence on Huntington, who learned to fiddle with Artie Look and Hollis Smith in the early '20s. In 1931, Gale Huntington (1902–1993) picked up the harmonica and began to play. "He [Look] was a tremendous natural musician and I learned most of my best fiddle tunes from him. We played for square dances all over the Island."[36]

"Over the years, Gale Huntington listened, learned and transcribed dozens of folksongs sung by the Tiltons."[37] Seven Tilton brothers made up the family of singers: William, Welcome, Edward Van Buren, George Fred, Zebulon, John, and Willard Earl. Keeping it in the family, Gale Huntington married Welcome Tilton's granddaughter Mildred in 1932.

"Benton (1889–1975) believed the essence of America was inherent in the folk music of the hills and valleys of south-Central United States. He feared that this unique music was in jeopardy of commercialization."[38] Thomas Hart Benton wrote and recorded local music whilst sketching the musicians who played it. He honed his ties to American folk music, capturing the musical prowess as well as the physical images of the musicians.

On the Vineyard every summer from 1920 to 1975, Benton opted for a bohemian lifestyle as a regular guest at Barn House and played with local musicians whenever possible. By the mid-1930s, Tom Benton and his Harmonica Boys proved a popular act. Rita, his wife, played both piano and guitar, while son Tom played the flute and mouth organ. The Bentons' social life revolved around music.

"Vineyarders kept the island's musical heritage alive by gathering for 'musical times' to sing old whaling and coasting songs after a day's work was done,"[39] wrote Annett Claudia Richter in her PhD thesis for the University of Minnestoa in 2008. "Dances at the town hall were enlivened by a three-piece orchestra or a gramophone. Gale Huntington, Ernest and Wesley Correllus, Hollis Smith and Mike Athearn sang and played, as did actors Ed McNamara and Jimmy Cagney."[40]

A memorable photo from this era "gives us the sense of the spontaneous and arbitrary mixture of both folk and classical music and instruments played at these gatherings, depending on what musicians came."[41]

Later, Benton, Woodie Guthrie, and Pete Seeger "traveled, wrote, performed, shared Martha's Vineyard and admired one another."[42] Ever the teacher, "We know that Benton also influenced Pete Seeger, in his early pursuits in folk music by teaching him folk songs on the harmonica at the Bentons' musical evenings in 1932."[43]

"It was the era when everyone seemed happy, the era when doors didn't have to be locked, the era of genuine good will."[44] As many as one thousand people gathered for services at the Oak Bluffs Tabernacle. It was a joyful time, according to many who were there.

Miriam Huss Williamson continued her recollection of those halcyon days singing in the Tabernacle during the 1920s. "Singing could be heard almost anywhere, almost any time in Oak Bluffs because half the members of the choir of the Tabernacle lived together, played together and loved to sing together wherever they were." The choir members were housed at the Camp Meeting Association headquarters, women on the second floor, men on the third. The Beatrice House served three meals a day all week for ten dollars.

She added, "The Tabernacle was crowded with folks, young and old, who sang lustily to the accompaniment of two upright pianos, an old foot-pumped organ, and the 32 or more voices of the Tabernacle choir. Even the noise of drenching rain on the corrugated iron roof couldn't drown the music."

Community sings on Wednesday evenings at the Tabernacle have been popular for more than a century. The weekly summer gatherings continue to this day, with young and old, men and women joining to sing hymns and popular songs. As Miriam Williamson recalled, "The 1920s were not the roaring twenties as I think about the summers on the Camp Ground. They were the musical, happy, singing twenties."

Music and dancing were not the only activities on the Vineyard in the 1920s. The waterfront was always a draw. Beaches were popular from one end of the Vineyard to another. Bathhouses ranged along Ocean Park in Oak Bluffs; nearby, the Highland Beach and the Inkwell were popular. Wherever the sea met the sand, bathers found their way to enjoy the ocean.

Across from the Tivoli was the Dreamland Dancing and Moving Pictures building, formerly a garage, later a popular movie theater, and today a popular dining site. Two bowling alleys held their own on Lake Avenue.

In the late '20s, Edgartown and Vineyard Haven opened golf courses, with Oak Bluffs not far behind. Summer visitors and locals enjoyed croquet and its variation Roque. Lawn tennis players had eight courts at Waban Park. Baseball unfolded there as well. Legendary third-baseman Pittsburgh Pirate Pie Traynor played from Cape Cod to Oak Bluffs before going on to the majors. Traynor was the first player from the Cape Cod League elected to the Hall of Fame; the second, and only other, was catcher Carleton Fiske of the Red Sox, in 2000.

The Edgartown Regatta began in 1924. Edgartown and Vineyard Haven Yacht Clubs opened. A specially designed sloop, the Vineyard Sound Interclub Class, was launched to level competition between participating sailors.

In the off-season, basketball was the game to follow. By 1925, all three down-Island high schools—Edgartown, Oak Bluffs, and Vineyard Haven—competed in highly partisan games through the winter months.

A silent movie, *Annabelle Lee*, was filmed on Martha's Vineyard and released in 1921. The film is based on the poem by Edgar Allan Poe but follows its own romantic theme, a romance set in the seaside community of Menemsha and Gay Head. As a German review noted, "Any resemblance of Herr Scully's film adaptation to Herr Poe's original poem is purely coincidental."[45]

The plot is simple. Annabelle's wealthy father disapproves of her suitor's working-class roots and requests that the couple separate for a year so they would (hopefully) come to their senses. David sails off into the sunset chasing rainbows while Annabelle lives in the family homestead, Pine Hill, filmed on the Vineyard's north shore.

Movie reviewer Brooks Robards noted, "Much of the pleasure viewers will find in the film comes from its footage of Menemsha Harbor in an era well before the 1938 hurricane that leveled the fishing village. Schooners sail in and out of the harbor before its jetties were built, and there are shots of many buildings, including the Gay Head lighthouse keeper's house, that no longer exist."[46] Scenes of the Gay Head cliffs make Vineyarders feel right at home.

The film recorded its action in iris shots, or circular matte. Director William Scully used title boards to move the story along, typical of silent movies. The film stars went on to act in other silent movies but never made it into the talkies, although Scully was an assistant director in talking movies.

Stills from the movie *Annabelle Lee* are housed at the Martha's Vineyard Museum, and a few are posted on the Steamship's *Island Home*.

Annabelle Lee may have been the first professional movie filmed on the Vineyard, but early home movies were also filmed on Island. To date, the earliest film uncovered was a drive through downtown Edgartown in 1925.

"The movie of Edgartown jounces and weaves down Main street, the camerawoman shooting from the front seat of a car whose hood ornament sparkles under the sun." So begins a description of a short home movie, filmed by siblings Bill and Clare Dinsmore.[47]

When still photographs were still rare, this video captured a moment in a key era, "at a moment in history that marks the start of modern Island resorthood."[48]

The footage is available online through Historic Movies of Martha's Vineyard, a program founded in 2012 by Tom Dunlop and John Wilson and organized by the *Vineyard Gazette*.[49]

The car bumps silently along Main Street in the film, and Tom Dunlop continues his review "where car and camera turn left. The film then travels north to the vicinity of the Harbor View Hotel before turning around and starting back the other way."

Items of intrigue are evident. North Water Street was two way, paved with scallop shells, sloppy and crunchy until crushed by traffic. Bailey Norton, the narrator of this reprinted silent film, was born in 1925. Norton noted that year-rounders walked on the harbor side of Water Street, while summer people strolled on the inland side, on the sidewalk.

Capturing a glimpse of unfolding history makes this a special ride down memory lane.

Another early film was shot by a photographer from the Fox News Reel, capturing the mating of heath hens. The plan was to show the film in theaters across the country. "The name of the Island will appear on the screen with these pictures, with the explanation that this is the only place in the world where the heath hen is found."[50]

The weather was perfect for filming on March 5, 1927, and "ten birds showed themselves on the field, of which seven were taken in a group." The four hundred feet of film consisted mostly of close-ups, "showing all the details of plumage, 'booming sacs,' and so on."[51] The film was to be shown on Island prior to release in national theaters.

We do not know if the film is extant. That several heath hens were filmed while mating, a few years prior to their extinction, lends a historic aura to the film.

In 1920...

Henry and Betty Hough became editors of the *Vineyard Gazette*. Charles Marchant, grandnephew of Edgar Marchant, founder of the *Gazette*, had edited the newspaper for more than thirty years. In a show of support, Marchant stayed on in an advisory capacity. He remained an advisor for ten years, until 1930.

7
IMMIGRATION

For ten thousand years and more, Native Americans have lived on Martha's Vineyard. Natives called the Island Noepe, which means "amid the waters" in the Wampanoag language.

For centuries, the Natives lived by the shore in the summer to fish and paddle in Vineyard waters. In colder seasons, they withdrew inland, to their wetus, which offered protection against winter weather. Based on archeological data uncovered at campsites and shell middens, Natives ate white-tail deer, fish, shellfish, and berries. Later, farming became a priority, with a focus on squash, beans, and corn. Theirs was a peaceful coexistence with nature through the seasons, living off and sharing the land, braving the ocean waters to catch fish or hunt whale, and surviving the challenges of stormy weather.

And then the white man came. Besides kidnapping a Wampanoag to show off the "savage" back in England, the white man brought disease, decimating the Island population by 90 percent. It has been estimated the number of Natives dropped from three thousand to three hundred in a century and a half. The white man imported his religion, his culture, his language, and his laws, compelling the Natives to adapt to his lifestyle. The white man proselytized the Calvinist ideology of the Congregational denomination of Protestantism, introducing the concept of the devil. The white man imposed European customs of dress, hair length, and money. And the white man squeezed the Natives into three communities: Chappaquiddick, Christiantown in West Tisbury, and Gay Head. It was in Gay Head where the white man eventually took the Natives' land, in 1871, in exchange for allowing them the right to vote.

The Wampanoag have not had an easy life with the white man on Martha's Vineyard over the past four centuries.

In September 1929, Lorenzo Jeffers was elected the new chief of the Wampanoag in Gay Head. Descended from his predecessor, Mittark, Jeffers intended to organize the tribe, "to gain representation in the Wampanoag Council, in which all the southern New England tribes with their branches were represented at a kindling of the council brand at Mashpee."[52] The Wampanoag had not formed a tribal council in centuries; this was big.

"Chief Jeffers plans big things for the next year," reported the *Gazette*. Specifically, Jeffers planned a tribal gathering in Gay Head. The new chief hoped hundreds or even thousands of "descendants of King Philip's warriors will gather at Gay Head." Plans called for three days of feasting and talks among tribal leaders and participants. (King Philip was the English name for Metacomet [1638–1676], chief of the Wampanoag Confederacy. Metacomet challenged English settlers encroaching on Natives in southern New England. The Vineyard Wampanoag did not take part in King Philip's War [1675–1676]; they sided with the white settlers on Martha's Vineyard, avoiding the ravages of war.)

In the spring of 1930, the *Gazette* headlined a story about "the first powwow to be held on Gay Head since the days of King Philip."[53] Jeffers was officially named chief of the tribe, and a great feast was held while "the flavor and spirit of those ancient days was revived."

Dressed in full Indian regalia, with a war bonnet on his head, "Rev. Leonard C. Perry of Fall River, Yellow Feather to members of the tribe," officiated at the powwow. Perry spoke eloquently and at length on Native American history, education, the future, and challenges faced by tribes in the current day.

The *Gazette* report continued: "Yellow Feather is the chief sachem of the Wampanoags, a branch of which he organized at Gay Head. He is descended from Massasoit and is tenth hereditary chief of the tribe." Yellow Feather passed the peace pipe with Chief Jeffers and adorned him with a war bonnet. This was the first time in 250 years such a ceremony had been celebrated among the Wampanoag in Gay Head.

The Wampanoag Powwow was the first tribal gathering in more than two centuries. *Courtesy of the* Vineyard Gazette.

During the evening activities, the following council officers were elected: Medicine Man, Harrison L. Vanderhoop; secretary, Mrs. Harry Webster; treasurer, Mrs. Helen Attaquin. The officers would be officially installed "with a revival of as much of the ancient Indian ceremony as feasible." By the time the powwow concluded, it was almost midnight. A sweet coda to the festivities was a shower held for a newly wedded couple: Jeremiah and Hattie Diamond.[54]

The Wampanoag are known as the people of the first light. They have always been here. The first white men came to the Vineyard in the early 1600s; many generations of immigrants from other countries have followed. "It shouldn't be a surprise that an island would attract islanders."[55]

Like the rest of the United States, Martha's Vineyard is a land of immigrants. In 1905, more than a quarter of the people in Oak Bluffs were immigrants. "By 1920, almost one-third of the Island's population were first- or second-generation immigrants. [By comparison, less than 10 percent of the Vineyard's current population was born outside the United States.]"[56]

Many immigrants came to the Vineyard from the Azores, Madeira, or Cape Verde, speaking their native Portuguese. When they arrived, they brought their family traditions and holiday celebrations with them. Many immigrants continued to honor their island of birth even as they settled into a new life on Martha's Vineyard. And many immigrants set up their own businesses, some of which are still around today.

Betty Alley (1912–2009) was born in Oak Bluffs on Vineyard Avenue, an area known as Little Portugal. Her parents were from St. George, an island in the Azores, the archipelago of nine volcanic islands one thousand miles east of Portugal in the Atlantic. Betty was the second of nine children. "As one of the older children, Betty naturally stepped into the role of helping her mother. 'When my mother had all her children, she never had any doctors or anything. She had them all at home, you know.'" Betty had to run across the field to her grandmother. "Come up to the house. Mother's having another baby."[57]

Betty embraced traditional Portuguese customs transplanted from the Azores. On Christmas Eve, neighbors walked house-to-house singing carols—in Portuguese—playing banjos and mandolins. The women enjoyed dancing the chamarita, a popular Portuguese folk dance, right in the street. Religion was a centerpiece in the Portuguese holiday tradition.

Betty graduated from Oak Bluffs High School in 1929, one of nine students, all girls. When she turned seventeen, her father handed her one hundred dollars; Betty grabbed her suitcase and off she went, by herself. She took the ferry to Woods Hole, where she caught the train to Springfield. There she earned a degree in business at Baypath Institute. Betty returned to Oak Bluffs and applied her bookkeeping skills to the town of Oak Bluffs and later to the extension service. She married and raised two fine sons, a true tribute to the community. Betty Alley is an example of first-generation people making a difference in the community.

For Joe Nunes (1910–2008) of Oak Bluffs, upholding Portuguese traditions and supporting the Portuguese community on the Vineyard were of great importance. He was always active with the Holy Ghost Society, serving as the president, and took on many roles in the annual Holy Ghost Feast. Along with friends, he planned and built the Portuguese-American Club in Oak Bluffs in 1930. For more than ninety years, the Holy Ghost Feast has been celebrated at the PA Club.[58]

Frank Peter Lopes (1905–1987) was a first-generation Vineyarder, son of natives of Faial in the Azores. Faial is a slightly smaller island in both size and population than Martha's Vineyard. Lopes and his father were professional gardeners. They sold flowers from their gardens on Look Street, Vineyard Haven, purchased in 1925. Frank Lopes's daughter Bernice shared memories with Chris Baer: "My father was able to speak, read, and write in Portuguese. He would read and write letters for some of their Portuguese friends." She added, "My dad was a well-liked person. He loved his family, loved working in his garden, he grew many different flowers and sold them in the front of our house. I think his favorite flower that he grew were glads."

"He gardened, fixed radios, even wrote a story about himself and a pet cow named Nellie. My grandfather had the cow, and it was in a barn behind Morrice Florist. The property was owned by my grandfather and is now owned by the florist."[59]

Portuguese immigrants made a home for themselves on the Vineyard. They acclimated to an island lifestyle akin to their land of origin and contributed socially and economically to their adopted land. Generations of hardworking immigrants enriched their new homeland.

In 1917, Congress enacted the first widely restrictive immigration law. The Barred Zone Act required a literacy test be administered to immigrants. Immigration officials had more latitude on whom to deny entry. Anyone born in the geographically defined Asiatic Barred Zone (China, Japan, and southeast Asia) was denied entry to the United States. Exceptions were made for the Philippines, as those islands are a protected territory. Chinese immigrants were curtailed by the Chinese Exclusion Act, and the Japanese prohibited their own people from emigrating. An even more restrictive immigration act followed in 1924, fostered by the belief in eugenics.

The goal of eugenics was to maintain and improve the genetic quality of the present population. In the United States, eugenics focused on curtailing immigration of those people deemed inferior and promoting white Anglo-Saxon Protestants. Eugenicists sought to preserve and protect what they considered the ideal homogeneity of the country for future generations.

Madison Grant's 1916 book *The Passing of a Great Race* implied that Anglo-Saxon immigrants worked harder and were more skilled than immigrants from southern and eastern Europe. Grant labeled the latter populations, primarily Jewish and Catholic, as lazy, ignorant, and uneducated. He made the baseless assumption that immigrants from such countries would not find it easy to assimilate into the American culture. So much for the melting pot.

Eugenicists participated in a congressional hearing that curtailed immigration. This led to the Immigration Act of 1924, known as the Johnson-Reed Immigration Act. This policy placed a quota on the number of immigrants allowed into the country in 1924, based on the 1890 national origins census. (In 1924, 2 percent of people from a given nation in the 1890 census would be allowed into the United States.) People from eastern and southern Europe were considered "inferior stock" and would dilute the influence, impact, and strength of the supposedly superior race, those people of Anglo-Saxon and Nordic descent. This theory would legalize and justify white supremacy.

Chinese and Japanese people were perceived to be the least desirable and thus prohibited from entry into the United States. Incest and anti-miscegenation (opposition to interracial marriage) laws were included in the 1924 act.

The justification for eugenics was expanded horrifically by Nazi Germany with the Holocaust. Nazis blamed the principle of eugenics on the United States because Congress codified the 1924 Immigration Act. Nazis used that act to justify the Final Solution of extermination of people of Jewish descent during World War II.

A tangential issue to eugenics and immigration was the work of Margaret Sanger, leader of the birth control movement and founder of Planned Parenthood. In Sanger's view, birth control could prevent unwanted children being born to disadvantaged parents or mothers with physical or mental limitations, which might challenge the newborn. It was feared such conditions would be passed to their progeny. Thus, even a constructive social service program such as birth control became entangled in the political chaos of eugenics and immigration in the 1920s.

IN 1920...
The circulation of the *Vineyard Gazette* was 600, slightly more than 12 percent of the Vineyard population of 4,800.

8
MIGRATION

In the early years of the twentieth century, thousands of Black families migrated north to gain economic opportunity and escape the scourge of racism in the South.

The Great Migration was a massive movement, a voluntary relocation of some two million Black southerners heading north, seeking opportunity in the workplace and freedom from the Jim Crow laws and disenfranchisement of the South. Black people rebelled against segregationist laws imposed by the Black codes, regulations imposed by White southerners limiting voting, housing, jobs, and social customs for Black citizens.

Economic opportunity lured southern sharecroppers away from their fields to northern factories. As thousands of (white) men enlisted in the army and went off to war, jobs became available for Black men in the industrial cities of the North. This migration had its greatest effect on midwestern and eastern cities, from Chicago and Detroit to Philadelphia, Boston, and primarily New York.

With restrictions placed on immigration, Black Americans found opportunity for their skills and talents in the urban North. This led to "a cross fertilization of Black people, Black arts, and the American dream."[60] Thousands of Black families moved from the rural South to the urban North, seeking social, economic, and political improvement.

Black families dreamed they would be welcomed in the North, that the prejudice and subjugation endured in the South would not be present in the

North. To some degree that was true, but political, economic, and social challenges still impeded equality between the races, even as a Black urban culture emerged in northern cities.

The Harlem Renaissance arrived on the heels of the First World War and continued into the late 1930s, just before the Second World War. The greatest number of Black migrants relocated in New York, specifically Harlem. As one commentator put it, referring to the artists of the era, "for every inch gained in Harlem, a mile was being traveled by Black people elsewhere in America."[61] The Harlem Renaissance was an uplifting experience for both artists and audience.

Black artists and writers who made the renaissance what it became shared and broadened the creativity that abounded in Harlem in this era. Artists developed their unique capabilities and worked with fellow Black creatives to expand the collective spirit engendered by this gathering of artists, writers, and performers.

The effect of the Harlem Renaissance was extensive and impressive. "As one of the most influential movements in African-American history, the Harlem Renaissance strengthened the foundation of what we have come to know as 'the culture.'"[62]

W.E.B. DuBois, founder of the NAACP, published *The Crisis*, a monthly magazine for the New Negro Movement, as the Harlem Renaissance was first known. Black patrons were welcomed at Shuffle Along, a jazz club on Broadway. Smalls' Paradise opened in 1925, "a cabaret that cemented Harlem nightlife," and was owned by a Black man, Ed Smalls, where Black and white clubgoers were welcome.

Jamaican American poet Claude McKay relocated to New York City in 1914. He connected with Max and Crystal Eastman, publishers of *The Liberator*. McKay served as co-editor of *The Liberator*, and it was in that journal, in 1919, that he published his most recognized sonnet, "If We Must Die," a reaction to the racial violence of murder and lynching of Black people known as the Red Summer.

Following his stint at *The Liberator*, McKay published *Harlem Shadows*, a collection of his best work, again featuring "If We Must Die," republished following the Tulsa Race Massacre of 1921. The next year, McKay traveled to the Soviet Union and met Max Eastman. McKay's novel *Home to Harlem*, published in 1928, was an important contribution to the Harlem Renaissance.

Martha's Vineyard enjoyed miniature versions of both the Great Migration and the Harlem Renaissance. Each unfolded differently from mainstream America. The Vineyard attracted a much smaller number of Black residents than urban areas, and those who visited Martha's Vineyard arrived at a small seasonal resort rather than a settled urban environment.

Adelaide Cromwell, a professor at Boston University with a summer home on the Vineyard, studied the growth of the Black summer community. Her analysis was based on a deep understanding of the movement of Black Americans, the migration if you will, to a new community. "The first Blacks at these places [summer resorts] were year-rounders, seeking work in the more favorable northern environment."[63] First, they formed a church, and then they built a school. The second group were summer people who came to work for white Vineyarders or came on vacation, staying at "guest houses and small hotels run by and for Blacks." The third group, vacationing as the leisure class, stayed at Black-owned hotels and then often bought their own homes.

Free Black people visited Martha's Vineyard in the mid-1800s, forming a Black enclave at Wesleyan Grove, the Methodist Campground founded in 1835. "There is, however, good evidence that there were occasional Blacks in attendance at the August Camp Meetings," Cromwell confirmed in her study of the growth of Black communities.

Recent research, in 2021, by Andrew Patch of the Martha's Vineyard Camp Meeting Association, indicates numerous Black vacationers summered in the Campground, beginning with Dr. Samuel Birmingham in 1862 and Reverend William Jackson in 1876. Both men, and likely others, purchased Campground cottages.

It wasn't easy. In 1889, Martha James, a Black woman from Boston, bought a Campground cottage to open as a lodging house. She was denied, and her house was literally towed out to Circuit Avenue, where her business succeeded.

Following the Civil War, when white families began to vacation on Island, they often brought Black servants with them. When those servants earned enough to vacation themselves, they sought out places to stay on the Vineyard. Often vacationers stayed with friends or at inns that catered to Black patrons in Oak Bluffs. Black families purchased Campground cottages along what was Wamsutta Avenue and Dukes County Avenue on the west end of the Campground, by School Street.

Beginning with Dr. Birmingham and Reverend Jackson in the 1860s and '70s to the turn of the century, Black families summered in the Campground. By 1904, however, Black residents had begun to be excluded, and their houses were literally removed, up School Street or into the Highlands. These Black residents were no longer part of the Campground community, which became a white-only settlement.

At the turn of the twentieth century, Black people purchased property where they were most welcome. And the Baptist Tabernacle in the Highlands, built in 1877, proved more welcoming than the Methodist Tabernacle in Wesleyan Grove.

Opportunities for Black vacationers were enhanced when the Tivoli Inn opened in 1899 on Circuit Avenue, operated by Louisa Izett and her sister Georgiana O'Brien. Also, Charles and Henrietta Shearer opened Shearer Cottage in 1912 in the Highlands, welcoming Black visitors to the Island. Both hostelries are extant.

Black people became a viable social construct on the Vineyard with Shearer Cottage and the Bradley Memorial Church. Hospitality and spirituality welcomed the Black populace. These two organizations, a hotel and a church, encouraged Black Americans to vacation and perhaps settle on Martha's Vineyard. The leaders of the two organizations, hotelier Charles Shearer and Reverend Oscar Denniston, stand out even today as providing a positive influence on Island life.

"There are times when forth-coming events cast their shadows before them, and one becomes acquainted with the motto of the Boy Scouts—'Be prepared.'" In 1913, the nascent Boy Scout motto was inserted into a news story on a surprise event for the local preacher, Reverend Oscar Denniston. He and his wife "were taken by complete surprise on Wednesday evening."[64] Prominent local leaders hosted an unannounced event in honor of Reverend Denniston, organized by Chaplain Madison Edwards of the Seamen's Bethel of Vineyard Haven. Thirty or more sailors attended the tribute.

Oscar Denniston was born and brought up in Kingston, Jamaica. He met and cared for a seriously ill visiting Vineyarder, Madison Edwards. The two struck up a lifelong friendship, and Edwards encouraged Denniston to move to Martha's Vineyard, which he did in 1900, acting on his faith that anyone who is willing to do hard work can succeed at virtually anything.

Reverend Oscar Denniston and family of Oak Bluffs. *Courtesy of Martha's Vineyard Museum and Doris Clark.*

And it was hard work that Reverend Denniston set out to do, serving as the minister to the Bradley Mission and pastor for sailors at the Vineyard Haven Seamen's Bethel.

Madison Edwards's tribute to Oscar Denniston advertised his success across the Island. Chairman of the Oak Bluffs selectmen Fred Smith said, "The town realized the good work Mr. Denniston has done and appreciated it."

Chaplain Edwards praised Denniston's work for his church in Oak Bluffs, the Bradley Mission, and for the "timely and kindly help brother Denniston has rendered at the Bethel." Over the past decade, he continued, "many of our boys of the sea have heard the gospel of truth from the lips of our brother and have started on the upward path. Reverend Denniston has helped me to a better and higher life."

Reverend Denniston acknowledged the accolades and said "he had not accomplished all he wanted to but has done a few things and was determined to go forward to higher accomplishments." He expressed love and support for the seamen. It was a signal event on Martha's Vineyard:

the recognition of a Black preacher for his work with local sailors and the congregants of his church.

Another tribute to Reverend Oscar Denniston occurred in 1927. The *Vineyard Gazette* observed that over the last century and a half, all the major improvements on Martha's Vineyard had been accomplished by the clergy. "And among those who toiled hardest," intoned editor Henry Beetle Hough, "and most alone will be the name of the Rev. Oscar E. Denniston, pastor of the Bradley Memorial Baptist church of Oak Bluffs."[65]

"At the time there was no Negro church on the Island, but what was known as the Oakland Mission was conducted on Masonic avenue by Mrs. Susan C. Bradley." The Mission was a small congregation, with only a couple of dozen congregants.

Denniston bought an old movie theater, the Noepe, a run-down building on Circuit Avenue, and, with little money, a lot of faith, and considerable work, converted it into a model of comforting hospitality for his parishioners. Pews came from an old Methodist church in Vineyard Haven, and a pulpit desk was donated by Boston's Old South Church. Denniston devised a welcoming atmosphere for his hundreds of followers, an integrated congregation from across the Island.

The *Gazette* praised the broad reach of the good reverend: "His fame as a preacher has spread and he has preached in many of the greatest cities of the country, where he has been received by clergymen of distinction and accorded many honors." Reverend Denniston stated his belief "that if a man is in deadly earnest, God and mankind will recognize and aid him."

In 2022...

"Rarely written about were the activities of the blacks, Portuguese or Indians—unless, that is, they got into trouble with the law," wrote historian Arthur Railton in the early twenty-first century. "Such discrimination in the news was not unique to the Island. All around the country, you had to read one of the black newspapers published only in the larger cities to find out what blacks were doing legally. When any mention was made in the mainstream press, the person being written about was always described as 'colored.'"[66]

9

RENAISSANCE

The opening of Shearer Cottage gave a strength and endurance to the summer community of this period, as had the leadership of Reverend Denniston to the year-round residents.[67]

The Harlem Renaissance blossomed in New York City. On Martha's Vineyard, the Black community bloomed with the work of Reverend Denniston of the Bradley Memorial Church. And the work of Charles and Henrietta Shearer expanded on Denniston's efforts to ensure that the Black community on Martha's Vineyard was here to stay.

Charles Shearer (1854–1934) lived a life from rags to riches. Born into slavery on a Virginia plantation, he was rescued by Union soldiers during the Civil War. Educated at Hampton Normal and Agricultural Institute, he met and in 1884 married Henrietta Merchant (1859–1917), a woman of African, white, and Native American descent and member of one of the oldest free Black families in Lynchburg, Virginia. Both Shearers worked at Hampton Institute in addition to teaching in a local elementary school.

In 1891, the Shearers moved north, part of the Great Migration, and bought a home in Everett, outside Boston. The young couple joined the Tremont Temple Baptist Church, one of the first integrated churches. The church had promoted abolition and advocated for civil rights. The Baptist religion was important to the Shearers.

Charles Shearer found employment as headwaiter in two prominent Boston hotels, Young's and the Parker House. The hospitality industry played an outsized role in the couple's lives.

Shearer Cottage was the most prominent hotel for Black visitors to the Vineyard in the 1920s. *Photo by Joyce Dresser.*

The Shearers heard of the Baptist Temple Park in the Highlands of Oak Bluffs and often visited the Vineyard to attend services. In 1903, they bought a home overlooking the park as a summer retreat. Henrietta Shearer opened a laundry service, catering to white families. In 1912, the couple expanded their house to a "twelve room seasonal inn, Shearer Cottage, operated in conjunction with the laundry. The inn catered to African Americans who, at that time, were not welcome at other island establishments."[68]

Shearer Cottage made an impact on the community. Shelley Christiansen continues her story of the Shearer family: "The Shearers provided lodging, meals, and catered events. The inn thrived. On any given day, the dining room was filled with fifty or more guests, socializing, and enjoying meals cooked by members of the Shearer family."

"Following rave reviews and word of mouth from two New Yorkers, spiritualist Harry Burleigh and Harlem politician Adam Clayton Powell, New York tourists and vacationers flocked to the Vineyard. Doctors, lawyers, businessmen, teachers and other civil servants followed. The Vineyard became a place to form friendships, see and be seen, savor the scenic atmosphere and enjoy the beaches."[69]

The horse and wagon used when Henrietta picked up or dropped off laundry now transported Shearer Cottage guests to and from Highland

Pier (by the present East Chop Beach Club). The laundry service was discontinued in 1917. "By this time, 1920, Shearer Cottage was very well known in the African American community both on and off Island. On Island, African Americans made up about five hundred individuals, or 10% of the population. Oak Bluffs itself was home to over one hundred African Americans, based on the 1915 state census."[70]

Adelaide Cromwell summarized the influence of the closely knit Black community in Oak Bluffs. The community was small, with only one hundred or so year-round residents, yet nearly five hundred Black visitors joined them in the summer. The Black community was a proud cohort, determined to enjoy the fruits of the Vineyard throughout the year. And the gradual merging of year-round and summer populations led to a community that included an agreeable melding of Black and white Vineyarders.

One woman who summered on Martha's Vineyard united the power of her singular talent—writing—with the arts of the Harlem Renaissance and the unfolding of the Black community in the Highlands of Oak Bluffs.

Dorothy West (1907–1998) was the only child of a progressive Black family from Boston. Her father, Christopher West, was born into slavery. "My father's dream was to be a wholesale merchant of fruits and vegetables in the venerable Boston Market. And so he was."[71]

Black families who had friends in Boston made the trek down to Martha's Vineyard and found a place to stay on the Island. They formed the foundation of the Black community. As a well-to-do family, the Wests followed their Boston friends to Martha's Vineyard. From the age of one, Dorothy West spent time on the Vineyard, initially at property along Oak Bluffs Harbor and later in the Highlands, on Myrtle Avenue, where her house stands today.

Dorothy West was precocious. She wrote her first story at the age of seven and was published in the *Boston Post* by the time she was ten. Finishing high school at sixteen, she attended classes at Boston University.

In 1925, eighteen-year-old Dorothy West moved to New York City with her cousin Helene Johnson,[72] a poet. When West walked through Harlem, she saw more Black people than she ever knew existed. This young Boston teenager joined the Harlem Renaissance and eagerly followed the throngs who encouraged the work of Black artists, writers, dancers, and musicians.

Poet Helene Johnson (*far right*) stands next to her cousin Dorothy West on a trip to Gay Head with composer Harry T. Burleigh. *Courtesy of the Martha's Vineyard Museum.*

West befriended a range of literati from the prominent poet Countee Cullen; to journalist and editor of *The Messenger* Wallace Thurman; to Zora Neale Hurston, author of *Barracoon*, the saga of the last slave ship to come to America; and poet Claude McCay, author of *Harlem Shadows*. Poet, novelist, and social activist Langston Hughes mentored West and nicknamed her "The Kid," as she was one of the younger artists in the movement.

West's 1926 story "The Typewriter" tied for second place with Zora Neale Hurston in a literary contest for *Opportunity* magazine, published by the National Urban League. And it was included in the literary anthology *The Best Short Stories of 1926*, along with essays by Ring Lardner, Robert Sherwood, and Ernest Hemingway. Other writing by Dorothy West appeared in the *Saturday Evening Quill*, a journal published by a writers' group West founded of the same name.

In her short story "Elephant's Dance," Miss West chronicled the Harlem Renaissance through the life of Wallace Thurman (1902–1934). "He was twenty-five and the Negro literary 'renaissance' was in its full swing. He wanted to get on the crowded lift and not get off till it skyrocketed him, and such others as had his ballast of self-assurance and talent, to a fixed place in the stars."[73] A dozen pages later, she wrote, "So Thurman lived and died, leaving no memorable record of his writing, but remaining as the most symbolic figure of the literary 'renaissance' in Harlem."

In 1932, Langston Hughes included her in a projected movie to be filmed in Russia about race relations in the United States. Black Americans were intrigued because Communists disapproved of the segregation practiced in the States. Although the film was never completed, West stayed in the Soviet Union nearly a year.

Dorothy West toyed briefly with a career on stage after a bit part in the play *Porgy*, but the written word proved her solace and salvation. With a literary agent, she began to publish stories in various periodicals. She had arrived.

Later, her short stories, novels, newspaper columns, and writing with young girls at the Inkwell in Oak Bluffs earned her a stellar reputation. That literary career was set in motion initially in the Harlem Renaissance and secured her place in Vineyard archives.[74]

Dorothy West recalled the Harlem Renaissance as a once-in-a-lifetime experience, a time when the optimism of her generation, her race, and her talent combined in a positive artistic form. And that form was recognized by those who appreciated the birth of a cohesive Black art and culture. The innocent naïveté of the Renaissance proved its guiding spirit, and the participants made the most of it, from art to poetry, from plays to short stories.

As the Harlem Renaissance began to fade in the mid-'30s, Dorothy West edited and published a periodical that promoted Black issues on social justice. *The Challenge* ran for three years, beginning in 1934. She was a

The plaque in front of Dorothy West's house on Myrtle Avenue in the Highlands of Oak Bluffs is on the African American Trail. *Photo by Joyce Dresser.*

contributor to the Federal Writers' Project from New York City, although she still considered Martha's Vineyard her refuge.

Dorothy West moved back to her family cottage in the Highlands after World War II and began her first novel, her most popular work, *The Living Is Easy*, published in 1948. For the next half century, she became a denizen of the Highlands, involved in theater, social organizations, and writing short stories and columns for the *Vineyard Gazette*. Her second novel, *The Wedding*, edited by and dedicated to former first lady Jacqueline Kennedy Onassis, was published in 1995 and later made into a Hallmark movie by Oprah Winfrey.

"Dorothy West of Oak Bluffs in her *Gazette* column was among the first to write about blacks in a 'white' newspaper without labeling them as such. To her, they were just people doing things, like everybody else. Skin color wasn't relevant."[75]

Dorothy West shared her passion for writing with Linsey Lee of the Martha's Vineyard Museum. "I think writing is a compulsion. If you want to write, you just have to write. You know when I am the happiest is when I am writing. When I write something good, sometimes I get so happy my eyes just fill up with tears."[76]

For a timeless memoir of the Highlands, Jocelyn Coleman-Walton's *The Place My Heart Calls Home* shares stories of summers at the beach, downtown Oak Bluffs, and adventures with family and friends. Her memoir savors summers later than the 1920s but offers a vivid view of Oak Bluffs in midcentury.

Two other books written by Black women worth reading are *Child Bride* by Jennifer Smith Turner of Martha's Vineyard and *Three Girls from Bronzeville* by Dawn Turner. Both are memorable. (The two authors share their last name but are unrelated.)

In 2022...

Today, Shearer Cottage functions as it has for generations as the backbone of the Highlands. Recently the Martha's Vineyard Commission approved an expansion from six to fifteen rooms. This is a major renovation for the historic Black hotel, owned by the Van Allens, descendants of Charles and Henrietta Shearer.

10

BARN HOUSE

One might surmise that the Roaring Twenties arrived on Martha's Vineyard aboard a steamship in 1918, motored inconspicuously up-Island, settled into an old barn overlooking Lucy Vincent Beach, and instituted a Communist takeover of the countryside.

The Vineyard version of the Red Scare was that a commune of off-Island liberals planned to disrupt the serene Chilmark landscape with socialist concepts and overthrow the tranquil democracy that was America.

Such was not the case.

In 1918, a collection of random intellectuals and artists from Boston and New York met at a cocktail party in Chilmark. They recognized amicable relationships with one another and decided to purchase property on the Vineyard so they could gather together again and engage in more lively conversation and convivial commentary. That was how Barn House began. The next year, some of these aficionados of the good life made pilgrimages up-Island to Chilmark, assessing available properties. They opted for what was known as the Mayhew Place, a rustic barn and late seventeenth-century farmhouse with outbuildings situated on forty acres overlooking the South Shore.

The deed for 451 South Road, Chilmark, was signed on May 31, 1919, by Gertrude King.

Barn House was born.

The focus of the collective initially and continually was the Barn, deemed the center of activity. While it lacked electricity, with minimal upgrade it served as a gathering site for the avant-garde group of artists, intellectuals, and businessmen. And when the Barn doors opened to the South Shore, sunlight warmed and brightened the dullest of conversations.

The first order of business, however, was to repair and modify the aging farmhouse, which did have electricity, followed by upgrading, to some degree, the nine primitive structures randomly scattered across the landscape, some quite distant from the Barn.

These tiny cottages were chicken coops, a mainstay of the old Mayhew farm, with neither running water nor electricity. One of the morning rituals was that "under every bed there was a potty and each morning members lined up, potties in hand, awaiting their turn to empty them into the bathhouse toilets."[77]

The first group of participants, numbering more than thirty, arrived in mid-August 1919 and eagerly settled into the various outbuildings. A cook, helpers, and a governess were employed to organize the amenities, such as they were, and ensure the wants and needs of the various members of Barn House would be met as much as possible. "Such a place, and such a life style, inevitably attracted 'free spirits.'" And that lifestyle, "some outsiders suggest, is at best a spartan adult summer camp with kids underfoot."[78]

Among early hosts and guests were journalist Walter Lippman, civil rights advocate Roger Baldwin, political cartoonist Boardman Robinson, and attorney/judge Dorothy Kenyon. Over the years, many more guests and participants would sign the guestbook and add artistic lore to the scrapbooks, expanding and glorifying the unique atmosphere inspired by the participants at Barn House.

The group held their Barn in the highest regard. Although the property was legally listed as Chilmark Associates, it was commonly called simply Barn House. The Barn served as a comfortable communal meeting place for cocktails, conversation, and amateur theatrical performances. It was the primary focal point for daily gatherings in the late afternoon, for drinks, food, conversation, and often a lighthearted skit after an arduous day soaking up the sun, sea, and surf along the south shore.

The Barn was a refuge, a place for the diverse group of individuals to gather and converse and cherish their time together. Art Railton continues his description of the Barn House clan: "Each afternoon at five o'clock, the group gathered in the barn, which was furnished simply but comfortably, for conversation and entertainment after a fun-filled day at the beach. It was widely said that they swam in the nude. Perhaps they did, but there are many photographs showing otherwise."[79]

Amusing skits were popular at Barn House. This sprite was photographed by the Gertrude and Stanley King family, members of Barn House. *Courtesy of the Martha's Vineyard Museum.*

Top: Guests at Barn House bunked in former chicken coops that lacked electricity and running water. *Courtesy of Martha's Vineyard Museum.*

Bottom: Chilmark's Barn House was a fixture of artists and intellectuals for generations. *Photo by Joyce Dresser.*

The dinner bell rang promptly at 7:00 p.m.

Members and guests paid a per-diem charge for the luxury of this relaxed lifestyle. They accepted assigned chores such as lawn mowing or painting. They endured, indeed relished, the rustic atmosphere and primitive accommodations.

"This group of well-to-do liberal artists, writers, and activists sought to adapt the property for use as a communal summer retreat."[80] Barn House served as a point of pleasure to enjoy the company of fellow artists and intellectuals. And it continues in operation as an artists' retreat.

Railton notes dryly, "During the 1920s, in perhaps the most ambitious project ever undertaken, members erected a water tower to provide water under pressure for the communal shower and toilets." Once completed, an adjacent windmill-driven pump filled the water tank from the nearby well. (Today, a great turbine stands high above the trees on nearby Allen Farm, generating power from the wind to run that historic sheep farm.)

Neither members nor guests at Barn House took themselves too seriously during their time together in this scenic setting. However, their working lives were serious, very serious. Mike Robinson was an outspoken liberal, even radical in his political affiliation. "Robinson's anti-capitalist and pro-union views...must have been an anathema to some Barn House founders." Yet at Barn House, he donned another hat, as a lyricist, an artist, a playwright. "Dorothy Kenyon's nephew Stanton was quoted as saying, 'We're all a little crazy here. At home, I'm a perfectly conventional fellow, but for some strange reason when I get here, something happens.'"[81]

Businessman Valentine Pulsifer, conservative Harry Kendall, and attorney Stanley King got along famously with radical cartoonist Mike Robinson while at Barn House. An unwritten expectation was that all convivial conversation, deep discussion, and silly skits were apolitical.

The postwar era was influenced by the Red Scare, when opposition to the First World War was linked to the overthrow of the Russian tsar and formation of the Communist government by the Bolsheviks, under Vladimir Lenin. (Red was the color of the Soviet flag.) Activist editorials were considered seditious amid mounting fears of the spread of Communism.

Conservative media raised alarms that immigrants would destabilize the American way of life. "The first Red Scare climaxed in 1919 and 1920, when United States Attorney General Alexander Mitchell Palmer ordered the Palmer raids, a series of violent law-enforcement raids targeting leftist radicals and anarchists. They kicked off a period of unrest that became known as the 'Red Summer.'"[82]

Barn House participants were aware of the political upheavals around them but used their time in Chilmark to savor the community of one another's company and the pleasure afforded by the seaside scenery. Sometime after their initial purchase, the cooperative purchased the Vincent Cliffs, just south of Lucy Vincent Beach, to expand access to the south shore. They did not want to continue to be beholden to Chilmark librarian Lucy Vincent, who owned the lovely beach. Over the years, members had been embarrassed to request her permission to frequent the shore, now known as Lucy Vincent Beach.

Locals were aghast at this contingent of radical liberals summering in their midst, presumably in the altogether. Talk among Chilmark neighbors ranged from horror to angst. Vineyarders assumed these unconventional off-Islanders came to Martha's Vineyard just to lie naked on the beach. Anxiety rose. Fear was expressed that these freedom seekers were free lovers, Communists intent on disrupting not just Chilmark's pastoral shores, but all of Massachusetts on their march to spread Marxism across the country.

The group did include a few guests with radical beliefs and progressive ideas, but many participants were stalwart conservative Republicans, more devoted to making money in profitable businesses than making mayhem with the status quo. In Chilmark, at Barn House, they were engaged in participating in humorous skits, amusing sketches, lively conversation, and a camaraderie that melded the various individuals closer over the years.

And alcohol.

Although the Eighteenth Amendment restricted the sale of liquor, there was no shortage of the prized liquid at Barn House. Vineyarder Craig Kingsbury was quite willing to supply illegal booze to this cluster of off-Islanders suffering from endless thirst but sufficiently swaddled in cash. Kingsbury brought "liquor from Oak Bluffs, where they had a bottling operation in the cellar of a hotel. One of the selectman [*sic*] was running things and it cost a dollar a quart."[83] Kingsbury claimed to provide the goods to meet the needs of this eager, cheerful, thirsty group of off-Islanders.

Barn House was a unique commune of like-minded intellectual activists who sought downtime in the remote reaches of Martha's Vineyard.

What could be wrong with that?

Participants at Barn House who did spark a social activist platform or a rebellious perspective in their speeches, writing, and organizational bias maintained a placid apolitical attitude among the staid and stalwart conservatives in their midst.

"An aura of mystery about Barn House members built up among year-round Chilmarkers. Who were these well-to-do off-Islanders who came to the Island on vacation, content to live in chicken coops and mix cocktails with politics in a barn? They certainly must be radicals, maybe even Communists, after all, that Marxist artist, 'Mike' Robinson, was one of them."[84]

In 1920...

Once Henry Hough eliminated competition by buying the *Martha's Vineyard Herald*, he hired staff to run the *Vineyard Gazette*. Joseph Chase Allen, a Vineyarder with a past, and Bill Roberts, a New Bedford printer, proved effective, efficient employees for decades. The Houghs purchased a larger press, which necessitated a larger office. The *Gazette* gained traction, but finances were not yet healthy.

11
RADICALS

In Chilmark, 451 South Road, aka Chilmark Associations, continued to flourish. The guest list from the early years resonated with liberal leaders of the era: Felix Frankfurter, Roger Baldwin, Norman Thomas, Walter Lippmann, and renowned artist Thomas Hart Benton. The participants thrived on an appetite of liberal thought.

Barn House participants avoided publicity. This raised the curiosity of their neighbors. Those who frequented Barn House were suspected of improper summer activities. Summer visitors virtually always remained down-Island, following a proper ritual; these off-Islanders stayed to themselves, swimming perhaps in the altogether and performing other unseemly activities.

Some of the "free spirits" are worth further mention.

Roger Baldwin (1884–1981) was a prominent pacifist, author, and one of the founders of the American Civil Liberties Union. He advocated for the Scopes Trial in 1925 and served as executive director of the ACLU until 1950. Baldwin was a guest, not a member, of Barn House, as he had his own Chilmark summer residence a mile or so away at Windy Gates, the former estate previously obsessively renovated by Lucy Sanford.

Felix Frankfurter (1882–1965) was chairman of a group advocating American support of the recently created Soviet Union in 1919. He helped found the ACLU in 1920.

The Palmer Raids were run by Attorney General Mitchell Palmer and overseen by J. Edgar Hoover, head of the Bureau of Investigation. Frankfurter considered the raids abhorrent because they randomly arrested suspected Communists.

Frankfurter called the Palmer Raids "utterly illegal acts committed by those charged with enforcing the laws." Hoover called Felix Frankfurter "the most dangerous man in the United States." Frankfurter served on the Supreme Court from 1939 to 1962. He was a guest at Barn House in the early years.

Norman Thomas (1884–1968) was a Socialist, pacifist, and six-time candidate for president. He was a Presbyterian minister and spokesman for Christian social activism. He was an advocate for the American Civil Liberties Union and a guest at Barn House.

Walter Lippmann (1889–1974) was a founding editor of the *New Republic* and pursued a career as a journalist and critic of American media. Lippman is considered one of the most influential journalists of the twentieth century. One of his key observations was that people do not care about public policy unless it affects them locally. He was a Barn House guest.

Boardman Robinson (1876–1952) was a cartoonist and painter. As a pacifist during the First World War, he traveled in Europe with John Reed and illustrated Reed's book *The War in Eastern Europe*.

Boardman's wife, Sally, called him Mike because of his interest in art. Mike was short for Michelangelo.

Robinson drew highly politicized cartoons for *The Masses*, the monthly magazine of Socialist conceits. *The Masses* was shut down when it was deemed in violation of the Espionage Act. Robinson later contributed to *The Liberator* under editor Max Eastman.

Mike Robinson was the creator of popular skits and theatrical programs that amused Barn House members. His short plays were lighthearted, apolitical, and humorous, memorable in that they included most of the Barn House audience.

Mike and Sally Robinson invited graphic designer Warren Chappell and his wife, Lydia, as their guests at Barn House. Chappell became a nationally recognized illustrator. At Barn House, Chappell was appreciated as a humorist as well as an artist. He easily generated a laugh from his cocktail companions.

Robinson's murals adorn the RKO building in Rockefeller Center and Department of Justice in Washington. He proved a dynamic influence on artist Thomas Hart Benton. "The painting of Boardman Robinson," wrote Martha Cheney, "and the propagandizing of Thomas Hart Benton were outstanding in keeping the subject [of mural painting] forward until the Federal Government produced its [New Deal] program."[85] Martha Cheney was the author of *Modern Art in America* (1939).

Thomas Hart Benton (1889–1975) was a Missouri artist and musician focused on regionalism. He summered in Chilmark in the 1920s as an early guest and prominent supporter of Barn House.

"Right from that first year, Tom [Benton] and his friends, virtually unknown, were accepted by those better-known artists and writers in that remote corner of the Island."[86] Barn House proved a stepping-stone for Benton. He brought his art student Rita Piacenza to Robinson's theatricals; they were married in 1922.

During the First World War, Benton worked as a camoufleur, applying camouflage paint to disguise navy ships. He painted shipyard scenes when he was in the navy. One of Benton's early paintings, *The Cliffs*, is an example of his experiments with the abstract art style of Synchromism, where color dominates form and expression. Benton painted naturalistic realism that came to be known as regionalism.

Benton once said, "The only way an artist can personally fail is to quit work."

Following the lead of Mike Robinson, Benton's first large commission, *America Today*, was a set of murals for the New School of Social Research in New York. In the ten panels, his focus was on the Deep South and the Midwest. His 1926 painting of Josie West, a Chilmark deaf mute, is one of his most iconic Vineyard paintings.

Siblings Crystal and Max Eastman represented not only the liberal wing of Barn House guests but also social activists on several fronts in the early twentieth century.

Their parents were ministers; their mother, Annis Ford Eastman, was the first woman ordained as a Congregational minister. With that parentage, the progeny knew no limits.

Sharing living quarters on 11th Street in Greenwich Village in the early 1900s, Crystal and Max set off on paths that sparked controversy in their efforts to enhance social, civil, and political rights. Each carved out a career of social activism across a broad range of issues, sometimes together, at times apart.

Crystal Eastman (1881–1928) was a frequent guest at Barn House in the early years. She was a feminist and a suffragist who assumed leadership in controversial issues early in the twentieth century. She was a social activist and an occasional Vineyard visitor. Her views and values advocated feminism, socialism, and civil rights.

Eastman rose to the pinnacle of Progressive reform with her book *Work Accidents and the Law*, which anticipated New York's Triangle Shirtwaist Fire. In the 1911 inferno, 146 young women perished. Victims' families received little or no compensation, which compelled states to support a drive for worker's compensation.

Eastman was a committed pacifist. In the groundswell of the First World War, Crystal Eastman sought to protect the rights of conscientious objectors. She was considered the founding mother of the American Civil Liberties Union. Other Barn House guests—Felix Frankfurter, Norman Thomas, and Roger Baldwin—were also credited with creating this civil rights organization. "From the very beginning, the ACLU counted among its founders, organizers, and supporters an impressive roster of women, many of whom were veterans of the fight for suffrage."[87]

Although she was actively involved in the support of the rights of free speech and protest, "Eastman is rarely credited with a founding role in what became the ACLU, for reasons that were bluntly gendered: In the crucial early months of the war, while the organization took shape, she was recovering from a difficult pregnancy."[88] Her son's birth precluded partaking in the formation of the ACLU.

"When the United States finally entered the war, in the spring of 1917, it ushered in a 'climate of compulsory patriotism' backed by a series of fierce crackdowns on free speech and assembly. The new Espionage and Sedition Acts brought thousands of people under arrest and surveillance by the nascent FBI, including the Eastman siblings, and forced the closure of *The Masses*, the magazine that Max had edited since 1912."[89]

During the Red Scare, Eastman was blacklisted, unable to work.

In 1918, Crystal and her brother, Max, founded the socialist magazine *The Liberator*, which published work by prominent writers from Ernest Hemingway and ee cummings to Helen Keller and Claude McKay, a leading force in the Harlem Renaissance.

The Nineteenth Amendment granted women the right to vote. Eastman was an advocate of suffrage, yet gave a speech titled "Now We Can Begin," seeking much more: "Now that the vote was won, women could say what they are really after; and what they are after, in common with all the rest of the struggling world, is freedom."

She encouraged suffragists to understand that equal rights should be the primary goal for women, not only the right to vote. Eastman wrote, "We must institute a revolution in the early training and education of both boys and girls. It must be womanly as well as manly to earn your own living, to stand on your own feet. And it must be manly as well as womanly to know how to cook and sew and clean and take care of yourself in the ordinary exigencies of life."

Eastman advocated equal pay for women and an end to employment discrimination. She co-authored the Equal Rights Amendment, which passed in 1972. The amendment had to be ratified by thirty-eight states; that succeeded in January 2020, when Virginia ratified the amendment. It still must be reapproved by Congress. The House passed the ERA on March 17, 2021, but faces a struggle in the Senate, which has yet to vote on it, as of February 2023.

Crystal Eastman was an advocate of a woman's right to choose, supporting Margaret Sanger, who coined the phrase "birth control" and founded Planned Parenthood in 1921. Eastman published "Birth Control in the Feminist Program," a magazine article in 1918. She argued that until women take control of their own bodies, they place themselves in a subservient role to men.

In her activist career, Eastman often founded and directed several organizations at once. Crystal Eastman was ahead of her time on many fronts.

Crystal Eastman divorced her first husband over his infidelities. (Her brother, Max, while married, had no qualms keeping his secretary as his mistress for twenty years.) Crystal Eastman married Walter Fuller in 1916 and had two children. In 1928, she succumbed to kidney disease at the age of forty-eight. Brother Max was devastated by her death.

"As an idealistic socialist—one commentator remarked that Eastman was usually the only feminist in socialist circles and the only socialist in feminist circles—she studied and wrote about socialist revolutions around the world."[90]

Max Eastman (1883–1969) lived a life promoting radical ideas, filled with controversy. He was involved in publications that challenged the status quo, from anti-war to birth control, from sympathizing with the Soviets to criticizing Russian rule. He critiqued the work of James Joyce. Max Eastman was a free spirit who opted not to have children yet coveted the affection of multiple women.

Max was named editor of *The Masses* in 1913, publishing the work of Carl Sandburg and Upton Sinclair, among others. The magazine became a mouthpiece for left-leaning editorialists, revolutionary in word and spirit. Editorials in *The Masses* opposed the United States entering the World War.

Eastman was arrested, accused of inciting activity against the federal government and being disloyal. The arrests were conducted under the Sedition Act of 1917. He was acquitted, but in 1918 *The Masses* was deemed in violation of the Espionage Act, as noted, for using the postal service to disseminate seditious material, and the publication was shuttered.

Eastman set forth on a two-year exploratory mission in the Soviet Union in 1922. He sought access to the interaction between Leon Trotsky and his successor, Joseph Stalin. Trotsky befriended Eastman. Upon his return to the States, Eastman published essays critical of Stalin's domination of the country; those essays earned Eastman verbal retaliation from Soviet leadership.

Max Eastman first visited Barn House in 1929 as the guest of Mike and Sally Robinson. In his autobiography, Eastman characterized the participants as "a tiny tribe or colony of writing and painting and thinking folk." Historian Arthur Railton observed that "the very radical Max Eastman...liked the Vineyard so much that he soon built a house atop a Gay Head hill, becoming one of the town's summer residents. His sister, Crystal, had been the Robinsons' guest at Barn House even earlier."[91]

After his Russian venture, Max and his wife, Elena, began "spending more and more time on Martha's Vineyard, where they fell in love with one location especially, Scitha Hill in the Lobsterville area of Gay Head."[92]

Using monies from his writing for *Reader's Digest*, they purchased the property in 1928. The Eastmans had the existing house torn down and built a studio for Elena and a comfortable home for them both. Max purchased adjoining acreage, some ninety acres. "Their new home, at 17 East Pasture Road, was in a section of the Vineyard that gave them what is still the best view on the island, shielded by scrubby trees, overlooking Menemsha Pond, and with access, albeit via a winding path and a now-crumbling boardwalk, to a private, pebbly beach."[93] (That winding path down to the shore is now accessible to the public, thanks to the Sheriff's Meadow Foundation, founded in 1958 by Elizabeth and Henry Beetle Hough of the *Vineyard Gazette*.)

Today Max Eastman's house serves as a creative writing retreat for faculty in arts and humanities at Indiana University–Bloomington.[94] *Photo by Joyce Dresser.*

In his autobiography, Eastman recalled a Barn House image of Stanley King, who later became president of Amherst College, "in a pair of blue trunks, standing on his head for five consecutive minutes, an achievement never rivaled, I believe, by any other New England college president." Eastman continued in his memoir: "It was a gay as well as a thoughtful crowd at the Barn House, and a wonderful introduction to the Island we were destined to love."

In 1969, Barn House observed a half century of operations as a cooperative summer camp owned by a group of intellectuals. "Barn House, that 'tiny tribe or colony of writing and painting and thinking folk' on the South Road in Chilmark, though thriving healthily through the years in a privacy not much differentiated from freedom, celebrated an occasion on Saturday which demanded mention in the public prints."[95]

Among the original participants who celebrated its golden anniversary were founder Dorothy Kenyon, Roger Baldwin, and their neighbor Lucy Vincent. Max Eastman's widow, Elena, savored her role as a special guest of the celebration. Kenyon recalled Mike Robinson as "one of our most beloved and colorful members. His red beard on the South Beach was something that, once seen, never could be forgotten."

The *Gazette* concluded, "Among the more or less privy secrets of Barn House is the graceful and gracious field which opens vistas of spaciousness through the widely opening doors of The Barn."

In 2021...

Comic Larry David, co-creator of *Seinfeld*, got into a brief but heated discussion with attorney Alan Dershowitz on the porch of the Chilmark General Store. The contretemps unfolded over Dershowitz's defense of the former president.

12
HISTORY

In 1921, trustees at the Vineyard libraries urged creation of a historical society to preserve and circulate literature about Martha's Vineyard. A Mrs. Shepard had collected a "valuable bibliography of Vineyardiana," as the *Gazette* phrased it, and sought cooperation among the town libraries to improve access and preservation of historical material. Dr. Charles E. Banks, a historian of note, served as editor at the initial meeting.

A second meeting to form an historical organization took place in March 1922. Then it was determined a countywide historical society should preserve and protect a permanent collection of literature and history relevant to Martha's Vineyard. Thus, the Dukes County Historical Society came into existence, with a goal to collect and publish historical material on occasion.

The society held an organizational meeting at the Oak Bluffs Library on October 23, 1922. Marshal Shepard was elected president, with Ulysses E. Mayhew as vice president. Bylaws were adopted for the organization, and dues were set at one dollar per year.

The group voted in favor of the society making temporary headquarters in Edgartown. The society remained in Edgartown until it relocated to Vineyard Haven, in 2018, renamed as the Martha's Vineyard Museum.

The society was charged with the preservation for perpetuity of varied articles, books, photos, maps, and manuscripts deemed important Vineyard historical records.

The Dukes County Historical Society, founded in 1922, was charged with preserving historical documents of the county. *Courtesy of the Martha's Vineyard Museum.*

Early in their research, members of the Dukes County Historical Society uncovered two Vineyarders who had overseen construction of the historic frigate USS *Constitution*. Colonel George Claghorn of Chilmark, a veteran of the Revolution, was the builder of record of the iconic vessel. His foreman was Prince Athearn of North Tisbury, a blockade runner in the War of 1812. Both men were skilled shipbuilders and mariners, as well as patriotic Vineyarders.

The ship was commissioned in 1794 and named by President George Washington. It was built at Hartt's Shipyard in Boston's North End and launched on October 21, 1797. Boston smith Paul Revere forged the copper fittings and bolts that secured the ship's hull, which consists of three layers of oak and pine, capable of repelling bullets and cannonballs, hence, "Old Ironsides."

Imagine! Two Vineyard men being responsible for building the *Constitution*, the oldest commissioned ship in the U.S. Navy.

The *Gazette* proposed a plaque be installed aboard ship to show how Martha's Vineyard played a role in the creation and construction of this historic frigate.

In more current news regarding the USS *Constitution*, Commander Billie Farrell assumed command of the historic vessel in January 2022. Farrell, a Kentucky native and 2004 graduate of the Naval Academy, said she was honored to serve as commander of "this iconic vessel that dates back to the roots of both our nation and our Navy and to have been afforded the amazing opportunity to serve as USS *Constitution*'s first female commanding officer in her 224 years."

It was noted, in 1922, that the inventor of the telephone, Alexander Graham Bell, had died. Bell had spent time on the Vineyard decades earlier, so it was natural his death would spark curiosity over his connection with Martha's

Vineyard. Bell explored the deaf community in Chilmark in some depth. He offered constructive assumptions about the inheritance of the genetic cause of deafness. Initially, Bell became involved in the concept of the telephone to assist his wife, who was deaf yet quite capable of reading lips. His mother, Eliza, became hard of hearing as a child, so she, too, was an influence on her son's invention.

"The third volume of the *History of Martha's Vineyard* by Dr. Charles Edward Banks gives lovers of the Island access to a store of valuable information and reminds them again how fortunate the Island is in its historian," extolled the *Vineyard Gazette* in 1925. This volume was eagerly awaited, coming more than a dozen years after Banks published the first two. And the book was published under the auspices of the Dukes County Historical Society.

The first two volumes of Banks's books recount the background of the six Island towns and major events in Island history. They are still valuable a century later. This third volume, "long anticipated and at last auspiciously published," focused on the genealogies of prominent Vineyarders. Volume 3 fit neatly beside its predecessors, with "the same attractive binding, the same clear, dignified type and excellent paper," the *Gazette* gratefully noted.

"Thus, we have in a few words characterizations of the Island's fathers, phrases which mirror their achievements, and, all in all, an unfailing bond between the listed names and the living history of the Island itself." The *Gazette* concluded, "The Island will always be in the debt of Dr. Banks."[96]

By the end of the 1920s, the *Vineyard Gazette* acknowledged the importance of the summer population, both seasonal visitors and day-trippers. In June 1929, the *Gazette* offered a Tuesday publication in the summer to bridge the gap of a week between Friday issues of the paper.

Editors Betty and Henry Hough believed that publishing the *Gazette* twice a week would be a boon to both seasonal visitors and businesses that sought to capture the summer crowd. The change was justified in response to Martha's Vineyard's prominence as a summer resort. The Houghs urged their readers to look for the *Gazette* twice a week in the summer months.

This expanded coverage in high season continued until 2013, when the *Gazette* reverted to a single Friday publication year-round but added an online version of the paper on Tuesdays.

Numerous social clubs were active on Martha's Vineyard in the 1920s. Groups for women included the Want-to-Know Club, the Garden Club, and the Triad Club. Since the 1950s, we can add the Cottagers of Oak Bluffs. For men, it was the Odd Fellows and more recently Rotary. These organizations were designed to improve the community and offer social and cultural outlets for their members.

The Want-to-Know Club was founded in 1893 in Vineyard Haven "to promote the social pleasure, intellectual growth and moral development of its members." Initially, membership was limited to twenty women.

Leigh Smith of West Chop twice served as president of the Want-to-Know Club. As she told Linsey Lee in 2017, "The Want-to-Know Club has been an active part in the lives of many Vineyard women for over a century." She went on, "I've always enjoyed the Want-to-Know talks."[97]

Want-to-Know Club meetings in the 1920s focused on the presentation of current topics of interest to women, ranging from women's suffrage to aerial navigation. On occasion, the talk was delivered in the form of a question, such as "Do business women make good wives?" or "Does the automobile promote sociability?"

"The devastating flu pandemic of 1918–1920 [was] apparently the only thing that could dent the early members' commitment to inquiry. In August 1918, they discontinued meetings until the following year because 'the times give less leisure for literary pursuits,' according to minutes preserved by the club."[98]

The Want-to-Know Club is still going after all these years.

The Triad Club of Oak Bluffs was founded in 1908. "Such clubs proved important cultural and social outlets for women whose lives were circumscribed by family, church and the expectations of women of the time."[99]

The three points of the Triad Club were to provide information, improvement, and sociability to its two dozen members. Meetings were tightly run, carefully memorialized, and included dainty refreshments. Dues were raised to one dollar per year in 1924. Meetings ran monthly from

The Triad Club picnicked at the down-Island waterworks in the late 1920s. *Courtesy of the Martha's Vineyard Museum.*

The mission of the Independent Order of Odd Fellows was to "visit the sick, relieve the distressed, bury the dead and educate the orphan." *Courtesy of the Martha's Vineyard Museum.*

October to May. Minutes from November 8, 1918, reported, "On account of the influenza epidemic the previous meetings were postponed."

Each meeting featured a talk by one of the members, nonpolitical, often patriotic. Lottie Hatch read "Women and the Ballot" in 1920. "The subject was cleverly handled and well written," according to meeting minutes. On occasion, a male guest was invited to speak; a few of such guests included Captain Ralph Packer, Joseph Chase Allen, Henry Beetle Hough, and H.N. Hinckley.

Other Vineyard women had projects and programs to keep them involved. The Martha's Vineyard Garden Club, the first conservation organization on the Vineyard, was founded in 1924. The membership list boasted eighty-five women the next year when the club met at Mohu, the Butler summer estate on Lambert's Cove Road. Participants appreciated a lecture about Boston's Arnold Arboretum, illustrated with colored lantern slides. The club had lobbied for removal of Island billboards and sought to improve the beauty of roadside views. It is going strong a century later.

Socializing is an important social element. Whether it's the Portuguese-American Club, a local church group, or a gathering of hunters, hikers, or fishermen, people enjoy getting together with like-minded neighbors and friends. That social community bond on Martha's Vineyard in the 1920s continues to this day.

In the 1920s...

Not every Vineyarder was enamored by the tourists flocking to the Island. "Some of us have formed a knockers' club this year," noted the *Gazette*. "If anyone asks us about the Vineyard, we say, 'We-e-ell, the mosquitoes were pretty bad this season,' or something of that sort designed to be discouraging."[100]

13

BUSINESS

Three children, all under eight, were waiting at the register inside Phillips Hardware, to make their purchases of penny candy. Watching them, I realized, once again, the import of a local business. Phillips Hardware is right there on Circuit Avenue, not just for a last-minute paintbrush or battery, but because it meets the wants and needs of all ages.

In the 1920s, as a clerk at Wigwam Hardware, John Phillips was turned down for a raise. Phillips was determined to be his own boss. "One day I was on my lunch break," he said. "I walked into this small hardware store called Island Supply and asked the woman working there if she wanted to sell. The next day we began to talk."

"When John E. Phillips (1906–1997) opened his store in 1928, penny nails were four cents a handful, a pound of putty was about a dime and every face that passed through the door was a familiar one."[101]

Phillips's parents emigrated from England to New Bedford, where they had the Hill and Dale grocery store. They then moved to Martha's Vineyard and settled in Oak Bluffs, where John's father worked as a butcher at Montgomery Square. In 1925, John was one of five Oak Bluffs students who graduated from the Oak Bluffs high school, across from the recently rebuilt town hall. John took the train to Boston to see about college. By the time he got to South Station, he had seen enough and took the next train back to Woods Hole. Phillips wanted to live and work in Oak Bluffs.

Phillips Hardware has been a mainstay on Circuit Avenue for nearly a century. The Oakwood Hotel building still stands above the store. *Courtesy of Donna Leon of Phillips Hardware.*

Left: Donna Leon and Susan Phillips run Phillips Hardware, a fixture on Circuit Avenue since 1928. *Photo by Joyce Dresser.*

Below: Christmas display in the front window of Phillips Hardware, a holiday tradition for all ages. *Courtesy of Donna Leon of Phillips Hardware.*

When Phillips bought the old Oakwood Hotel, the store found its current home. (The second and third floors of Oakwood had small guest rooms. The only bathroom was on the second floor. Today, the upstairs is used for hardware storage.)

Phillips Hardware has always been a family operation.

Initially, John's wife, Evelyn, worked for the telephone company in Vineyard Haven, then joined her husband at Phillips. Their son, Robert (1933–2015), worked for his father as a teenager. In 1984, he took over with his wife, Pauline. The hardware expanded through the generations; today it is run by John Phillips's granddaughters, Donna Leon and Susan Phillips. Their brother Ken worked at the hardware for many years. "We grew up in the store," said Susan.

A family business is a family enterprise. The sisters' husbands, Jaime Leon and the late James Cage, spent time behind the counter, as have Donna's children Heather, Michelle and Chris. Grandchildren, cousins and even second cousins know their way around product displays. Robert Phillips was very proud of his family and their dedication to the store through the years.

Phillips Hardware has successfully adapted to change. Robert Phillips was "proud of the way the business has been able to change in response to consumer culture." The late Jack Shea wrote in the *MV Times*, "Listening to the history of the business is akin to watching snapshots of the changes in American's retail trends." Robert Phillips noted, "You more or less have to pay attention to change."[102]

Phillips Hardware once sold candles that were salvaged from the *Port Hunter*, the supply ship that sank off East Chop in 1918.

Today, selling paint is very different from in 1928. The old way to tint a color was to add it manually; today it's by computer. In the '20s, the paint-shaking machine might loosen the top of the can, which could lead to a Jackson Pollock panorama. Today, the shaking can is enclosed.

Saws and drills were simple hand tools in the 1920s; today, they are electric or cordless.

Back in the day, a customer would have to verbally explain what was needed; today, cellphones allow customers to share a photo of what to replace.

The aisles of Phillips have an ageless quality. In the holidays, Susan and Donna set up their antique Christmas display in the front window to cheer passersby.

John Phillips enjoyed children who visited his store at Christmas. He had a hidden intercom inside a stuffed Santa, where he could listen and speak to children. The kids thought Santa was talking to them. That's how this local business won the hearts of its youngest customers.

Vineyard businesses run by immigrants cater to the whole Island population, as well as their own. Besides Phillips, several businesses have survived since the early years in the twentieth century.

Brickmans was established as a cobbler shop in 1913. The business modified over the years and now sells footwear, popular apparel, and even toys. Richard Clark ran the sporting goods operation at Brickmans. When the need arises, the store rents out tuxedos.

Charles Vincent opened a general store selling tobacco and candy on Main Street Vineyard Haven, also in 1913. Today, Gary and Robyn Sylva run the business, known as Mardell's Gifts & Jewelry, a gift shop with greeting cards and tchotchke galore.

Early in 1917, the four Cronig brothers saved enough money to open Cronig Brothers Market, initially a meat market with its own slaughterhouse, situated on the corner of Main and Church Streets in Vineyard Haven, now the site of Rainy Day.

"We bought a wagon for $10 and a horse for $30, and we opened," Henry Cronig recalled in 1964. "It was a sorry-looking store. We piled everything we had on the shelves in order to make the best showing possible."[103]

Edwardo and Maria Giordano opened their restaurant in Oak Bluffs in 1930. Seating thirty-five people, the bistro was initially in the old Pawnee House across from the post office. They baked pizza in an old wood oven, insulated with sand, lit in the morning with kindling, then coal added for the proper pizza temperature. A small pizza cost fifteen cents; a large pizza was two bits (a quarter).

Giordano's expanded over the years, purchasing the Magnolia Restaurant in 1943 across from the Flying Horses. In 1984, Frank, Peter, and Heidi Dunkle renovated the building, installing Victorian décor with stained glass and raised paneling, upgrading the woodwork. Giordano's is a seasonal restaurant in the heart of downtown Oak Bluffs.

Antonio daRosa emigrated from the Azores as a child. He founded Martha's Vineyard Printing Company in 1935; today, his son Tony runs daRosa's. *Stan Lair collection, courtesy of Chris Baer.*

In 1935, Antonio G. daRosa opened Martha's Vineyard Printing in Oak Bluffs on the second floor of the Herald Drugstore, in what is now Reliable Market. In 1940, Antonio purchased 46 Circuit Avenue, and the business morphed into daRosa's and has been there ever since.

In 2017, Antonio's son Dennis recalled, "He became the Island's only commercial printer. Printing was a labor-intensive business. It took 15 minutes to print a box of envelopes. Now that takes about three at most. My father worked hard. My mother used to have to tell him to come home to eat."[104]

Sons Tony and Dennis ran daRosa's for years. Dennis passed away in 2020; Tony keeps the printshop printing, a mainstay on Circuit Avenue for nearly ninety years.

The sign outside Jim's Package Store reads 1929, toward the end of the Prohibition era. The site served as Lake Avenue Garage when Alpha Leonard purchased it from Edwin Frasier in the early 1920s. Leonard's two sons, Freeman and Howard, as young men, worked at what became Leonard's Motor Services and Sport Shoppe from the 1920s through 1966. The business was sold to Arthur BenDavid and family, who renamed it BenDavid's Garage.

Eddie BenDavid ran the liquor store into the 1980s. He shared a photo of his father and uncle behind the counter; another person in the picture is Jim Pratt, presumably of the eponymous Package Store. Incidentally, the word *package* came from having to cover or package alcohol so it would not be visible in public.

Jim's Package Store dates to 1929. Pictured here are *(left to right)*: Jim Pratt, Arthur BenDavid, a manager, and Gus BenDavid. *Courtesy of Eddie BenDavid.*

The Mansion House, originally opened in 1769, was sold in 1922 to George Heeley, a hotelier from Providence. The historic Vineyard Haven hotel has been known for generations as one of the more popular hotels in the southeastern corner of Massachusetts. Emeline Look managed the Mansion House for half a century, and on her passing, her family sought a new owner to assume management of this iconic hostelry.

Susan and Sherman Goldstein purchased the Mansion House in 1985 and run it today with their children, Josh and Nili. It's a family enterprise, maintaining a long-standing Vineyard tradition.

In April 1929, construction began on the new Tisbury School. Stakes were posted and excavation was underway. Forms would be built, cement poured, and soon the workmen would commence the laying of bricks. A Mr. Cottrell, manager of the construction, assured the press that no off-Island labor would be imported unless there was no alternative. (As of this writing, portable classrooms fill the playground and construction of a new Tisbury school is underway, more than ninety years after the original building was built. The school is estimated to cost $82 million; it is due to open in February 2024. Fingers crossed.)

Healthcare is a priority everywhere, but especially on an island seven miles out to sea. In 1922, a local house was converted into a hospital in Eastville, Oak Bluffs.

"Martha's Vineyard Hospital Has Brilliant Opening. First Operation Is Successfully Performed." The banner headline said it all. An open house

Parade down Circuit Avenue. The 1920s was an era of celebration, complete with marching bands. *Courtesy of Phillips Hardware.*

drew the curious: "Inspection of the rooms seemed to be the first interest of all visitors. The transformation of a dwelling house into a most homelike and pleasant place for the sick was what we saw already accomplished. The result must have been a source of pride to the workers."[105]

The news report continues. "Upstairs are the operating room, the babies' room, the resident nurses' room and other private rooms, and a five-bed ward." The new hospital was ready for patients. More details followed: "The first operation was successfully performed Wednesday morning when Miss Goldrick of Oak Bluffs went under the knife for appendicitis. Dr. Mathewson performed the operation, assisted by Dr. Worth and Dr. Mayhew."

Six years later, in 1928, a completely new hospital building was designed to meet the expanded needs of the growing community. "Ultimately the hospital will have the finest equipment that money can buy and although not all of it will be provided at once allowance has been made in the plans for an ideal hospital development."[106]

Ground was broken in the autumn of 1928 for the new hospital in Oak Bluffs. Expected cost was $81,000. No completion date was shared with the press.

Three wings made up the new facility. The medical surgical wing was to the left; the wing to the right was the male ward, with windows that overlooked the harbor. The rear section housed the women's wing, kitchen, nurses' area, and general lavatory and toilet. The women's wing did not overlook the harbor but faced south, for the warmth of the sun.

Three outside telephone connections were installed: central hall, kitchen, and office. A call system encouraged silent communication, with no buzzers or bells.

The *Gazette* article explained the finer points of the new structure: "The fireplaces and mantels will be of colonial design in keeping with the character of the building." The facility will have "no ornamental work, strictly speaking, the domed central hall with arches, the mantels and other details will give the building a colonial beauty and it is expected to be strikingly attractive and appropriate."

The hospital would be dedicated to "the World War heroes of the Island as a living monument," according to the *Gazette*. (In 2010, one wing of the original 1929 hospital was torn down when the hospital was completely rebuilt and renovated at a cost of more than $40 million. Work was completed in 2016.)

"The Vineyard, particularly Vineyard Haven harbor, because of its location half-way between New York and Boston, has always been favored by vessels seeking shelter from storms or any service from the land."[107] Ships sought refuge or supplies in Vineyard Haven after journeying up or down the East Coast or from overseas.

On occasion, sailors who had contracted a disease easily transferred to the Vineyard shores. Smallpox was frequently transmitted, causing numerous epidemics over the years. In 1763, the first hospital on Martha's Vineyard opened in Holmes Hole, for victims of smallpox. A second hospital opened in Eastville in 1796 and a third in 1866 on the Edgartown-Vineyard Haven Road. Another marine hospital was added in 1879.

The newest Marine Hospital, the imposing building that overlooks Vineyard Haven Harbor and now serves as the Martha's Vineyard Museum, was built in 1894.

"When the hospital was a unit in the Marine Hospital Service, the officers wore uniforms and carried a sword at inspection."[108] Attendant staff wore uniforms, and the discipline, rules, and inspections of the hospital were enforced as if it were an army facility.

In 2019, the Martha's Vineyard Museum relocated to the former Marine Hospital in Vineyard Haven. The "temporary" location in Edgartown lasted ninety-seven years. *Photo by Joyce Dresser.*

By 1930, the Marine Hospital was "conducted as civilian hospitals are, but with additional privileges added, all of which makes the place more comfortable and homelike for its inmates." However, a key requirement, the *Gazette* noted, was that "those patients who were able were required to assist in keeping the wards cleaned." It's doubtful if such a policy would be very popular today.

Midway through the 1920s, the Western Union Telegraph Company assumed operation of the telegraph lines of the Martha's Vineyard Telegraph Company. Since 1908, the Vineyard telegraph company had run the lines between the Vineyard and Nantucket. Now Western Union, a much larger corporation, managed services between islands.

Companies are absorbed theoretically to provide more efficient service and reduce costs. The news in 1926 was not that different from mergers or acquisitions today. Intriguingly, it was noted an unspecified disagreement had been festering between Western Union and the Martha's Vineyard Telephone Company. The good old days were not immune to their own angst and anguish.

Henry Beetle Hough worried about the standardization of design in Vineyard houses. "The old houses of the Vineyard have repeatedly given against the invading commonplaces of off-Island building design. The old houses of the Island embody such a simple, beautiful and eminently suitable sort of character and craftsmanship."[109] Hough sought to keep things as they were, for life to stay the same, or at least show respect for the earlier architecture on the Vineyard.

Henry and Betty Hough used their mouthpiece of the *Vineyard Gazette* to slow down modern ways and development on Martha's Vineyard. They wanted to keep tourists coming with their bulging wallets yet preserve the basic fabric and fragile tranquility of the Island. Development meant replacing natural formations by substituting man-made structures. "There is room here for untold summer sojourners of the future, for new fleets of yachts and for new estates of broad acres. But the new should be introduced with due respect for the old."[110]

In 1920...
"To earn extra money, in 1923 Henry and Betty left the paper in the hands of their new associates and returned to New York City." With financial support, the *Gazette* survived. "It was three years before they finally thought they had enough for their newspaper's coffers and happily returned to their $12.50 a week income from the *Gazette*. They were back on the Vineyard again in the spring, just in time to see the apple trees blooming."[111]

The *Gazette* served as their lifelong commitment.

14
TRANSPORT

The dawn of the modern era was most evident in transportation, on land and sea and air.

It was marked initially by the demise of trolley service on Martha's Vineyard in 1918. Horse-drawn trolley service began in 1872, bringing Methodists from the Highland Pier, now the site of the East Chop Beach Club, to the Camp Meeting Association, along with their trunks, trinkets, and paraphernalia. The most famous passenger was President Ulysses S. Grant, who rode the horse-drawn trolley on his 1874 Vineyard visit.

The Martha's Vineyard Railroad ran from Oak Bluffs through Edgartown and out to Katama from 1874 to 1895. It was that year, 1895, that trolley cars were converted, virtually overnight, to electric service and the horses put out to pasture. Trolley service continued through Oak Bluffs and across the Lagoon to Vineyard Haven until 1918. (A 1913 Eldridge map of the Vineyard included a trolley line out to Chilmark, but that never got beyond the talking stage.) When trolley tracks were torn up in 1918, the rails were melted down for munitions in the war effort. After a half century of service, the trolley was no longer the most efficient means of transportation.

A small section of track is embedded in the pavement outside the headquarters of the Martha's Vineyard Campmeeting Association, all that's left of the trolley tracks.

Automobiles supplanted the trolley, slowly at first, but by 1920, there were hundreds of cars motoring along Vineyard roadways.

In 1923, a question was posed: "How many cars are on Martha's Vineyard?"

William Manter owned the Dukes County Garage at Five Corners. He compiled a survey of various automobile models on Island, by town, and shared it with the public.

Unsurprisingly, Manter found the fewest cars in Gay Head, only 31, and the most in Tisbury, 214. There were 56 vehicles in Chilmark and 205 in Oak Bluffs. Edgartown had only 91 cars, comparable to West Tisbury with 86. The *Gazette* editorialized, "West Tisbury seems to have enough automobiles to carry all the people at one time while Edgartown probably would have to make three trips. Quite interesting."

A graph gives the following number of people and cars per town on the Vineyard in the 1920s:

Gay Head (Aquinnah)	161	31
Chilmark	252	56
Edgartown	1276	91
Oak Bluffs	1333	205
Tisbury	1541	214
West Tisbury	270	86
Total on the Vineyard:	4,833[112]	683

The survey found 683 cars on Martha's Vineyard as of March 1923. With a population of 4,833, that averaged 1 car for every 7 people.

As for the various makes of automobile, Ford led with 382, followed by Buick at 125 and Dodge with 34. Other manufacturers included Hudson, Maxwell, and Reo, at 10 each, with Chevrolet, Packard, Essex, and Cadillac at the bottom of the list.

Leonard's Motor Service and Sport Shoppe sold Hudsons on the site of Jim's in Oak Bluffs. Renear's sold Fords on Church Street, Vineyard Haven. And William Manter of Dukes County Garage sold Buicks and Chevrolet. The automobile was here to stay.

As more automobiles arrived on Island, the streets across Martha's Vineyard were upgraded and paved. In 1921, the Edgartown–Vineyard Haven Road was paved, and North and South Roads were completed a decade later. Now Vineyarders could motor from town to town much easier than in the days of horse and buggy or trolley.

William Manter sold Buicks at the Dukes County Garage at Five Corners, 1923. *Stan Lair collection, courtesy of Chris Baer.*

In mid-August 1929, a traffic light was installed at Monument Square (now Farland Square) in downtown Oak Bluffs, adjacent to today's information booth. This was the first traffic signal approved for the southeastern part of the state. Five streets converged at this intersection and bore the bulk of Vineyard traffic. Officials explained they sought to eliminate confusion by splitting cars into different routes to make their way through downtown Oak Bluffs.

To improve traffic flow, increase visibility, and reduce distraction, the statue of the Union soldier was removed from Monument Square to the corner of Ocean Park, where it stands today. An overhead beacon was mounted atop the traffic signal to guide airplanes from Boston or the Cape to the Katama Airfield in Edgartown.

Trucks, jitneys, and buses now met the needs of Vineyarders. Cronig's Brothers Market showed off its new Reo grocery truck for Island-wide deliveries. George Athearn delivered vegetables and fruit up-Island in his 1919 vintage truck, now the property of Bink's in Oak Bluffs. This primitive pickup features an electric starter instead of a crank. The whistle on the exhaust was an add-on feature; when the truck goes downhill, the driver can blow the whistle, which sounds like an approaching locomotive. That would be a surprise.

Jitneys, or small buses, offered taxi service, far from the trolley lines. Jitneys were owner-operated vehicles hired to take people where they wanted to go—think early ride-share Uber options.

Summer tourists and Island visitors sought mass transport. Horton's Reo buses began service in 1922 and operated throughout the decade. Passengers could board the bus at the old trolley waiting room in Oak Bluffs (now Dipping Donuts by Jim's Package Store) and ride to Tilton's Drug Store (now Claudia's Jewelry) on Main Street Vineyard Haven.

Hortons Buses took tourists up-Island to Gay Head, twenty miles, promoting early motorized commercial tourism. Harry Horton himself often drove school groups on field trips to the Gay Head cliffs. Another sightseeing service, Vineyard Line Tours, began operations in 1923, out of Vineyard Haven. Competition improved business.

In the mid-summer of 1923, the launch of the newest steamship to serve Martha's Vineyard was announced. The *Islander* was the first of four popular vessels, known as the White Fleet, added to serve the Vineyard in the 1920s.

The *Islander* met the needs of the expanding tourist trade, as the vessel doors were large enough to accommodate large vehicles. It could handle up to twenty-six cars. This was the first Vineyard ferry specifically designated to accommodate automobiles.

The *Islander* was also the first steel-hulled vessel constructed for the New Bedford, Martha's Vineyard and Nantucket Steamship Company by Bath Iron Works in Maine. For its size, the *Islander* was the fastest ship to be built of any comparable vessel at the company: nine months.

The new ferry boasted a crew of fifteen and accommodated two thousand passengers. For added comfort, the saloon deck was enclosed, as was the freight deck. Passengers had the option to sit in one of fifteen private staterooms, equipped with writing desks, pen, and ink.

Two coal-fired boilers generated steam to propel a single screw propeller, speeding the *Islander* across Vineyard Sound at up to fourteen knots. The *Islander* drew fourteen feet of water.

Following the launch of the *Islander* in 1923, three more ships were added to the White Fleet in the 1920s. The *Nobska*, built in 1925, held 1,200 passengers; cars were loaded on the side of the vessel. The *New Bedford* was launched in 1928 and the *Naushon* in 1929.

To align the four new steamships of the White Fleet with their ports of call and add confusion to what was going on, two vessels—the *Islander* and *Nobska*—had their names changed to the *Martha's Vineyard* and the *Nantucket*, respectively.

One amusing incident occurred when a gravestone was loaded on a freight cart. During the especially rocky crossing, the cart began to roll from side to side of the *Islander/Martha's Vineyard*. The crew grew fearful of spiritual activity on the freight deck, but nothing untoward occurred.

The *New Bedford* slid smoothly off its ways at the Quincy shipyard and prepared to join its sister Vineyard steamships. The *New Bedford* was the third of the four new vessels of the White Fleet. Its lines resembled her sister ships, though the main freight deck was longer, which provided a third more space for freight. The ferry accommodated up to thirty-five of "the largest automobiles." Two turntables expedited loading and unloading vehicles, although they still had to be driven through the side of the vessel, then turned sharply. Passenger capacity was two thousand.

The name *New Bedford* was a first for the steamship line. Now all its vessels bore names aligned with their port of call. The *New Bedford* was launched in May 1928, in time for the summer season.

It was noted that the smoking room and the men's lavatory were in the rear of the vessel, which necessitated the lunchroom be removed to the saloon deck. The new ship had the capacity to make ice and serve cold water.

The *New Bedford* took most of the crew from the vessel it replaced, the *Uncatena*. The *New Bedford* ran between Edgartown and New Bedford. The *Islander/Martha's Vineyard* was the early morning boat out of New Bedford, while the *Nobska/Nantucket* was the early morning boat from Nantucket. It was a different world in the 1920s.

The *Naushon*, Queen of the Island Fleet, was launched in 1929. It boasted thirty-two staterooms with hot and cold running water. *Stan Lair collection, courtesy of Chris Baer.*

The *Naushon* was nicknamed the Queen of the Island fleet when it was launched in 1929, now the largest of the fleet, stretching 250 feet. Writing desks had monogrammed stationery, as befit the queen.

The White Fleet was unique in the history of Vineyard vessels: there was uniformity of design and function. The company determined to modernize its steamships and succeeded admirably. All four of the White Fleet excelled in service over the years. Two decades later, two of the ferries, the *Naushon* and the *New Bedford*, were taken over by the U.S. Navy during World War II for service overseas as troop transfer and hospital ships.

During the 1920s, the steamship company rebuilt the wharves in Oak Bluffs, Nantucket, New Bedford, and Woods Hole.

To cut corners during the early years of the Depression, the New England Steamship Company painted all four vessels gray so workmen would not have to repair or cover rust spots. Public outcry was swift: the White Fleet should be white. Very soon it was.

The first airplanes touched down in Oak Bluffs Harbor on July 15, 1919. Two navy hydroplanes flew across Nantucket Sound from the Chatham Navy Air Base. The purpose of the trip, the *Gazette* explained, was to "spur recruiting for the service and to let people see how the airplane funds have been spent."

Ten days later, two wealthy New York stockbrokers, Melvin Fuller and Myron Brown, both of whom had summer homes on East Chop, planned a secret flight from New York City to the Vineyard. Pilot Griffin managed to reduce the train and steamship fifteen-hour trip to three and a half hours by air, including a stop on the Cape for fuel. Their secret was out by the time their hydroplane landed in Oak Bluffs Harbor. "Hundreds on the shore of the island cheered and waved handkerchiefs. It was a new era introduced to the summer colonists."[113]

The hydroplane, "a Curtiss flying boat, of the latest type," cost $18,000. The only incident of note was a punctured pontoon, repaired without delay.

"The coming of the commuters by air has excited this island and its hundreds of summer residents and vacationists as never before," raved the *Gazette*.

Passengers interested in a flight were offered the opportunity at $10 a head. (That would be $160 with inflation today.) "Two persons sat in the forward open cockpit with an unobstructed view of the Island from heights few had ever experienced." The *Gazette* report continued exuberantly: "On one flight, the passengers were Eugene O'Neill, a guest that weekend of Mrs. Henry Hand of East Chop, and Miss Priscilla Hand. The *Vineyard News* called O'Neill 'a promising playwright from Provincetown.'"

"'A promising playwright,' indeed. The following year, O'Neill's first full-length play, *Beyond the Horizon*, was awarded the Pulitzer Prize for drama." Playwright Eugene O'Neill, who went on to write *Long Day's Journey into Night*, *Anna Christie*, and *Desire Under the Elms*, earned extra money as a local journalist on the Cape and Vineyard as he refined his playwriting chops.[114]

The flight from New York intrigued people across the Island. Vineyarders were excited to have the chance to go for a ride in the hydroplane. More than sixty people took advantage of the opportunity, enjoying a unique adventure.

A dinner party for the participants in this novel event was held at the Wesley House, orchestrated by Eugene O'Neill. From the dinner party, the group segued on to the Tabernacle, where thousands gathered to hear stories of the adventure of this flight from New York City. This event signaled the dawn of air transport on Martha's Vineyard.

Katama Airfield opened in 1925. The hard clay surface of the grassland plain was ideal for the nascent airplane. The runway did not absorb rainwater, so the field was never too wet to land or take off.

Within two years, daily newspaper delivery service was offered on Island. Flights from Boston to Katama began in 1927 and continued until the stock market crash, two years later. The flight from Boston took an hour; a round trip flight was twenty-five dollars. Vineyarders considered this Boston connection even more impressive than aviator Charles Lindbergh's flight across the Atlantic that year.

In 2020...

A count of freight trucks riding steamships between Woods Hole and Martha's Vineyard was just under fifty thousand. The Island is dependent on ferry service for virtually all necessities.[115]

15

WRECKS

Accidents and incidents on the steamship line are extremely rare, even though Vineyard Sound is a busy shipping route. When two steamships collided in a dense fog off New Bedford Harbor in 1922, it was news. Big news.

The steamers *Miramar* and *Gay Head* crashed into each other, and the latter was seriously damaged. The prompt reactions by both veteran captains prevented more serious damage. There was one injury; a man suffered a bruised leg.

Both vessels were sounding their fog horns, but the fog was opaque, so neither vessel was visible to the other. It proved impossible to avoid the collision.

The steamer *Gay Head* sustained damage to its wheel box amidship. Captain Sandsbury anchored his vessel to assess the damage, and the *Gay Head* was taken out of service for repairs. The *Miramar* was smacked hard but, with less damage, managed to continue from New Bedford on to Woods Hole and thence to Vineyard Haven. In the meantime, the *On Time*, no relation to the current Chappaquiddick ferry, was put into service, to keep the Vineyard linked by steamer to the mainland.

Another shipwreck was reported: in a thick fog, "eight men, and perhaps others, paid the toll in a tragedy of the sea in Vineyard Sound last Friday morning."[116] Coastguardsmen from Cuttyhunk and Gay Head witnessed a ship in trouble but were unable to reach it in time. A suitcase, an ice chest, and a life preserver with the name "John Dwight, New York" were salvaged from the site of the sunken ship.

It was assumed that the *John Dwight* had recently received a cargo of alcohol from a mother ship. Anchored in Vineyard Sound, without lights to avoid detection, the *Dwight* was rammed and sunk by another vessel in the thick fog. Or perhaps it was intentionally sunk.

"The burning of the steamer *Sankaty* at her wharf in New Bedford on Monday evening of this week, has been the most thrilling event in this section this week."[117]

The 1924 conflagration destroyed the steamship. The fire began in bales of hay stacked on the dock of the New England Steamship Company, destroying the dock and burning the *Sankaty* down to the waterline. Damage was estimated at $350,000, nearly $6 million today.

Five crew members aboard the flaming vessel had to leap into the harbor to save themselves. The fire was contained to the steamer and the dock itself. However, once the mooring lines burned through, the tide floated the flaming *Sankaty* across the harbor, "where it touched the *Charles W. Morgan*, the famous old square-rigger."[118] Fortunately, the Fairhaven Fire Department was able to extinguish the blaze and protect this last American whaleship. Built in 1841, today the *Charles W. Morgan* is safely moored at Mystic Seaport.

Coming on the eve of the Fourth of July weekend, the fire caused problems for steamship customers.

A strong summer storm tore along the coastline of Massachusetts in the late summer of 1924. Hurricane-force winds wrought havoc in Vineyard Haven and Edgartown Harbors. Reports from across the Island noted uprooted trees, damaged crops, and destroyed buildings caused by the ferocious wind. This August storm was deemed the worst in a half century, except for the notorious Portland Gale of November 1898.

This storm proved the death knell for one of the last of New Bedford's square-rigged whaling ships, the *Wanderer*. It was driven onto the shoals off Cuttyhunk and wrecked in the nor'easter. Seven members of the crew were rescued by the Cuttyhunk lifesaving station; another eight crew members reached safety on the *Sow and Pigs* lightship. The *Wanderer* was a total loss.

While this was intended to be the final whaling expedition of the famed *Wanderer*, it was acknowledged that the price for whale oil and whalebone no longer justified the dangers and costs of whaling. Science had moved forward; whaling was no longer a financially viable business.

"The sinking of the *Kershaw* by the Dollar Liner *President Garfield* has been described as one of the most spectacular collisions ever witnessed in New England waters."[119]

The ocean liner *President Garfield* plowed into and sank the freighter *Kershaw* off East Chop, Oak Bluffs, on June 1, 1928. Seven crew were trapped and died when the freighter sank on a clear, calm evening, as the vessels intended to pass each other in Vineyard Sound.

Like the 1923 sinking of the *John Dwight*, the sinking of the *Kershaw* made the *New York Times*.

Like the 1918 sinking of the *Port Hunter*, this was a case of missed communication.

"The stars were shining, the moon was bright and the water was hardly rippled by wave or swell. Yet, with visibility estimated at 10 to 15 miles the two steamers collided!"[120]

"The collision is said to have occurred during a confusion of signaling, under a bright moon that provided clear visibility for ten miles."[121] Each vessel clearly saw the other prior to the crash. Signals were exchanged, and according to shore witnesses, both ships carried the proper lights and lookouts. The collision was apparently caused because of a miscommunication of whistle signals. Both crews testified that the other did not give the proper signals.

"The *Garfield* passed Nobska and West Chop Lights and was headed for Hedge Fence Lightship," the *New York Times* explained. The freighter was clearly outlined by the bright moonlight, about four miles distant. The *Garfield*, steaming along at fourteen knots, blew one blast of its whistle, meaning it would pass the freighter on its port (left) side. The *Times* piece

SEVEN OF CREW LOST IN SHIP COLLISION

They Were Trapped in Kershaw, Struck Off Cape Cod by President Garfield.

CHINESE CREW SAVED 29

Word that the freighter *Kershaw* was rammed by the liner *President Garfield* in Vineyard Sound made national news. *Courtesy of the* New York Times.

concluded: "It is alleged that her [*Kershaw*] course was then changed to cross the *Garfield*'s bow."

Despite an exchange of signals and clear visibility, the two vessels collided. The bow of the *Garfield* struck the freighter. The crash sent the *Kershaw* pilothouse overboard with three men inside. The captain and two mates managed to scrabble onto the floating wreck and were rescued.

Seven crew of the *Kershaw* were trapped below and drowned.

The crew of the *President Garfield* rescued twenty-nine men from the sinking *Kershaw*. Once the collision occurred, Dr. George Hand boarded a local fishing smack (a large, rigged fishing vessel), the *Leona*, of Oak Bluffs. He checked out the survivors at the Marine Hospital in Vineyard Haven. The rescued crew were sent on to Boston.

"The seven who drowned were trapped in the engine rooms and firehold." CG 147, a Coast Guard vessel, searched the waters of the collision but encountered no more survivors.

An officer aboard the *President Garfield* compared the sound of the collision to the crushing of a thousand cardboard boxes.

Constructed in 1899, with four decks, the *President Garfield* was on the final leg of its fourteenth round-the-world cruise. Most passengers and cargo had been discharged in New York, and the *Garfield* was bound for Boston with three passengers. One of them, Mildred Slater of Belfast, Maine, was quoted as saying, "It was not so much like the meeting of two strong objects, as it was the strong hitting the weak."[122]

Cora Fisher of Oak Bluffs was sitting in a car near the steamship pier. "It was like a strange dream," she said. "The moonlight was shining brightly, and I could see both ships come together very plainly. I just couldn't believe my eyes. When I heard the thunderous crash a few seconds later I knew it was true....Never had I felt so small and helpless."[123]

Thinking the freighter might capsize, the captain of the *Garfield* held the *Kershaw* afloat until it sank. Meanwhile, the *President Garfield* emptied its fuel tanks to raise her bow. Within five minutes of the collision, the *Kershaw* bow rose "up into a convulsive twist" and sank, stern first, "carrying seven of its crew to their doom."

To protect the shipping line from underwater debris, the plan was to blow up the remains of the sunken freighter in December 1929. It cost $88,000 to dynamite the *Kershaw*, over $1 million today. The twisted steel was scattered across the ocean floor in an area as large as a football field. Today, divers can descend sixty to ninety feet to view the remains of the *Kershaw*, with fifteen feet visibility. The area is near a shipping channel, so care is advised, especially in the summer months. Two boilers from the wreck attract tautog.

The collision occurred near Hedge Fence shoal, near the crash site of the *Port Hunter* and tug *Covington* ten years earlier, in the middle of the night in the middle of Vineyard Sound.

Survivors of the *Kershaw* were brought back to Norfolk, Virginia, while the *Garfield* turned back to New York to repair its damaged bow. Immediately after the collision, shoes, typewriters, and bed coverings surfaced from the wreck amid a great oil slick from the *Garfield*'s fuel tanks.

Later that June, a body washed onto what is now State Beach. It was assumed to be from the *Kershaw*, although positive identification could not be made.

Within days of the collision, the owners of the *Kershaw*, Merchants and Miners Transportation Company, filed a $750,000 lawsuit against the Dollar line of the *President Garfield*, claiming the cruise ship "was not in charge of a competent person."[124] A dispute arose over the cause of the crash, as it was a clear night and both vessels were properly illuminated. The ships had each changed course, and it was contended that signals blown by the *Kershaw* had drowned out the liner's signals, so the freighter was unaware of the *President Garfield*'s whistles.

A collision occurred in 1932. The steamships *Martha's Vineyard* (formerly the *Islander*) and the *Nantucket* (formerly the *Nobska*) met by accident in Vineyard Sound. The two ships were supposed to pass each other, but in the dense fog, neither captain caught sight or sound of the other. One of the two hundred frightened passengers suffered a minor injury in an incident none would soon forget.

This was not a serious collision but served as an admonition that accidents are unpredictable and continue to occur, even in the best of weather conditions and with proper safety warnings in place. The ocean can be a dangerous means of transport.

In 2022...

Martha's Vineyard is still an island. Vineyarders live with steamships that break down or do not run because of high wind, which makes docking difficult. Fortunately, there have been few collisions, groundings, or fog disruptions in recent years. Safety pays. However, mechanical issues continue to plague steamship service.

16

PROHIBITION II

Brazen tales from the rumrunning days continue to surface, decades after the repeal of Prohibition.

The wreck of the *Allaha* on Noman's Land is a nautical tale shrouded in mystery. The *Allaha* was a fifty-foot speedboat rumored to be a rumrunner. Shortly before Christmas 1926, the *Allaha* was south of Noman's Land when the weather turned. "A howling northeast gale set in. The men, putting on all speed, steered for the island, but the buffeting of the wind and waves was too much for the *Allaha*." The vessel sat low in the swells, began taking on water, and proved difficult to steer. "They missed the opening and crashed into the rocks and spikes which are all that remain of the pier. The men reached shore in safety and were cared for at the farmhouse."[125] Machinery and fittings were salvaged from the *Allaha*, but the hull of the speedboat was destroyed by the fierce ocean waves. That was the end of the *Allaha*.

Was it a rumrunner? Did the crew ever salvage the cargo? What was the backstory? We may never know what really happened on that Christmas wreck on Noman's nearly a century ago.

A year later, on April 23, 1927, off Squibnocket in Chilmark, Gay Head Coast Guardsman Raney, aboard CG 282, set out to assist a grounded vessel, the *Etta M. Burns*, lying low in the water, apparently with a cargo of fish. No crew were aboard, but two men were in the vicinity. The men innocently claimed the *Etta M. Burns* was headed to New York's Fulton Fish Market when it ran aground in thick fog early that morning.

Initially, illegal booze was shipped in wooden boxes until canvas sacks proved more expedient. *Courtesy of the Bradford Tavern.*

The story got fishier when the captain, Frank Rice, could not be located. Coast Guardsmen sought to float the vessel by pumping the bilges of the *Burns*, but the two crew members demurred. Coast Guardsman Raney grew suspicious. "I returned to the vessel and began a careful search of her. No papers could be found. The hold was apparently full of fish." His report grew more illuminating. "My suspicions were aroused, and I began digging under the ice. About eighteen inches below the surface, a piece of canvas was found. Beneath this was a cargo of liquor."[126]

The Coast Guard set up a guard on the *Etta M. Burns*. Heavy seas pounded the ship. Bottles of liquor began to roll in on the surf of Squibnocket beach. "Vineyarders—quickly aware that a rumrunner was aground and that booze was floating out of her—gathered on the shore. Most of them were there to see whether they could pick up a few bottles."[127] Free booze. Rolling right in to shore on the waves. Who would object?

The exception to the curious bystanders was a local man, Chester Poole, an ardent advocate of Prohibition. Poole took matters into his own hands by wading into the waves and smashing every bottle he found in the water or on the beach. Much of the cargo of the *Etta M. Burns* never made it into a cocktail glass.

Years later, *Black Ships*' author Everett Allen, then a teenager, along with a dozen or so peers, thought it would be great sport to set fire to the remains of the *Etta M. Burns*, decaying on the Squibnocket shore. "The old schooner did not burn easily or quickly in the beginning, but suddenly what we had done was out of control." Nervous at their success in setting the ship afire, Allen added, "We formed a useless bucket brigade."

Tracking the column of black smoke to the teenagers, the Chilmark fire chief arrived. He opined that the burning of the *Etta M. Burns* was "neither safe nor sensible." Everett Allen forever regretted his participation in torching the *Etta M. Burns* with his mates from the Baptist Sunday School class of Vineyard Haven.

The effort to curtail the rum trade was a constant challenge on many fronts. When a rumrunner was arrested, he often gave an alias, possibly the name of an acquaintance. On one occasion, more than twenty men were apprehended; they all gave the same name.

There was always a chance bribery could save a rumrunner from arrest. Coast Guard personnel could be persuaded to form an alliance with a captured rumrunner for a bit of cash. Or the Coast Guard would seize the contraband for their own use or possible sale.

Midway in the decade of Prohibition, as many as 160 supply ships, mother ships laden with alcohol, fanned out up and down along the East

Coast, legally lying a dozen miles offshore. This was the infamous Rum Row. Hundreds of powerboats, speedboats often disguised as fishing boats, motored within that twelve-mile limit between the coast and Rum Row. Each month an estimated 100,000 cases of liquor were brought ashore. The Coast Guard was severely outmatched.

The Coast Guard estimated their patrol boats seized only about 5 percent of the illegal alcohol being transported to the shore and sold to bootleggers. In response to their plea for additional support to hunt down rumrunners, President Coolidge sought an appropriation of nearly $14 million from Congress to purchase and upgrade Coast Guard vessels and equipment, doubling their five-thousand-man force. Stakes were raised.

Frank Butler of Martha's Vineyard was a worthy adversary of the Coast Guard. He was one of the more successful rumrunning skippers, operating both fishing and speedboats on his liquor runs. Rumrunners often installed an old airplane engine in their boat to outrun the Coast Guard. Butler designed a double-bottom boat to conceal his illicit cargo from prying eyes. Another innovation was to pour dirty engine oil over the exhaust manifold, creating a dense black cloud of smoke to obscure a getaway.

"Frank Butler never made any bones about telling the world what he was up to. He had been a fisherman all of his life and one day he was fitting out a new boat." Asked how many pounds of fish his new boat could hold, Butler didn't hesitate: "About seventy-five cases."[128] Author Everett Allen continued, "The whole rumrunning business lent itself to extraordinary feats of seamanship, to intrigue, mystery and cunning."

The *Nola* was Frank Butler's steel-sheathed speedboat, the one he used to transport liquor from Rum Row to the shores of the Vineyard. For five years, he had successfully used the *Nola* in his rumrunning operations.

"Five years to the day after her launching, December 18, 1931, *Nola* began the run through Vineyard Sound; there were, in fact, three patrol boats and a destroyer, whose skippers knew she was coming and who were determined to catch her if they could."[129]

The armor-plated *Nola* rounded Gay Head and entered Vineyard Sound. Coast Guard vessel 813 was in pursuit. But the Coast Guard's bullets bounced harmlessly off the plated *Nola*. Frank Butler, the *Nola* skipper, was confident he could outrun the Coast Guard as usual. The Guard added two more patrol boats, the 405 and the 2297, to the chase.

The *Nola* was laden with booze. Butler had taken so much on board that five-gallon tins of Belgian rum had to be stacked up on deck. In plain sight. Butler was determined to outrun the Coast Guard, and he would have succeeded, had not the tins of liquor proved an easy target for sharpshooting Coast Guardsmen. All it took was one bullet to ignite one tin; the alcohol burst into flames, and the *Nola* was soon fully engulfed.

That single shot caused the fire and subsequent explosions.

Unable to escape, Butler brought the *Nola* to a halt. The race was over. The 813 pulled alongside and rescued the crew of the flaming vessel. A destroyer approached and tried to tow the *Nola* to a safe harbor to salvage the confiscated alcohol as evidence of illegal activities. A series of quick explosions caused the vessel to sink, taking the incriminating booze to the ocean floor.

As Chris Baer summarized the tale, "Notorious rumrunner Frank Butler of Chilmark was shot through the wrist by a Coast Guard machine gun when the armor-plated, liquor-laden speedboat he captained was fired upon and sunk in a wild 1931 nighttime chase off Nomans."[130]

The Coast Guard radioed a request for an ambulance to meet the 813 at the Vineyard Haven pier as one of the *Nola* crew, Butler himself, had been shot and required medical attention at the Marine Hospital (now the Martha's Vineyard Museum).

The Coast Guard was relieved to capture Frank Butler, a man "long sought for liquor-carrying activities." And in a simple twist of fate, the vessel CG 813, which brought down the *Nola*, was a former rumrunning speedboat itself that had been captured by the Coast Guard and converted to a patrol boat. "As a rumrunner, the 813's name was *Tramp*—and Frank Butler had been her skipper."[131] You can't make these stories up.

"The rumrunners had better and faster boats than their government pursuers, in many instances, but one advantage that the Coast Guard did have was the ability to intercept and decode the smugglers' radio transmissions."[132]

One of the more diligent rumrunner radio operators was an anonymous fourteen-year-old boy who spent a summer on Nantucket during Prohibition. He was radio savvy. Three men set him up to communicate information and coordinate locations between small rumrunners and their larger supply ships lined up along Rum Row. The unnamed teenager did what he was asked and never got caught. "The guys took good care of me. My bosses were off-Islanders, from Boston. If you didn't blab and behaved yourself, if they took you under their wing, they'd protect you. I sent so much money home."[133]

He added, "There is a code of ethics. You know; the skippers of the boat know you, but you never say anything. Not even now, you don't, after all this time." Born in the early 1900s, the man, then well along in years, confided to the author of *Black Ships*: "You never say anything. Not even now."[134] *Black Ships* was published in 1979, decades after Prohibition was repealed by the Twenty-First Amendment. That teenage radio operator still held his tongue.

~

On occasion, the Coast Guard managed to break a rumrunners' code, using their radio to contact the mother ship or even the bootleggers on shore. In October 1932, toward the end of Prohibition (it was repealed the next year), the *Amacitia* was some thirty miles south of the Noman's Land buoy, trailed by the Coast Guard, which had broken the rumrunners' code.

The Coast Guard was in control. Witnessing activity aboard the *Amacitia* and monitoring its radio communications, the Coast Guard moved in and arrested the crew of two dozen men. The final transmission from the vessel was, "The Coast Guard is here." The Guard seized $160,000 worth of liquor in canvas sacks and a couple of small boats. It was an impressive haul, worth over $3 million today.

The captain of the *Amacitia* never knew his radio code had been deciphered.

~

Geoff Currier extolled Vineyarders' propensity to avoid the law in his article commemorating a century since passage of the Prohibition amendment. "In fact, the Vineyard hosted enough bootlegging, rumrunning, moonshining, and other Prohibition-era activities to merit its own film, 'Bootleggers on Martha's Vineyard—Craig Kingsbury Talks about Prohibition,' produced by Linsey Lee and Kate Feiffer. You can see it here: bit.ly/MVbootleg."[135]

Craig Kingsbury told Linsey Lee, the Martha's Vineyard Museum's oral historian, "Hey, when Prohibition was going good, be a hard job to throw a rock and not hit on a booze establishment somewhere [on the Island]." Research librarian Bow Van Riper of the museum believes the Vineyard was evenly split between the wets, who favored alcohol, and the dries, who supported Prohibition. Currier added his final thoughts: "For the purpose of this article, I chose to concentrate on the rumrunners who supplied the liquor—they had more vivid stories to tell. To tell the stories of people sitting around abstaining from alcohol would be—pretty dry."

"There came the day when all of this ended, accompanied by a holiday atmosphere, a national sigh of relief, certain regrets from the smugglers, some of whose trade sputtered on for a few years more, and generally, quick forgetfulness of an era of American history that had produced high adventure for many, money for some, and death for others."[136]

The Eighteenth Amendment was repealed by the Twenty-First Amendment at 3:30 p.m. on December 5, 1933. In Boston, as well as across the country, clubs, bars, and package stores "undertook a regal celebration which rapidly assumed New Year's Eve proportions."[137]

The end of Prohibition was celebrated around the country. *Courtesy of the Bradford Tavern.*

In some cases, the repeal of the Eighteenth Amendment was not that big a deal. "When the depression hit and Franklin Delano Roosevelt was elected president, the 18th amendment was repealed. The Island hardly noticed the difference."[138] Life continued, but with less illegal activity and a sense the Vineyard was able to move on to deal with other issues of concern.

"Rumrunning is the stuff of which history is made and elusive history at that; it remains one of the nation's best-kept secrets." Prohibition offered the hint of real danger as well as the possibility of a handsome reward, unintended consequences of the Eighteenth Amendment.

In Bill McCoy's obituary, in 1949, the *New Bedford Standard Times* recounted McCoy's exploits with the *Arethusa* off Noman's Land back in 1921. The *Times* challenged the purity of his liquor, which he claimed to be "the real McCoy." The newspaper reported that the bottles purchased from Bill McCoy by reporter Earle Wilson, who had been disguised as a fisherman, were, according to the chemist's report, nothing more than "cheap rotgut whisky and rain water."

Concluding his engaging account of rumrunning off the East Coast in the days of Prohibition, Everett Allen wrote, "America has not really decided whether the seagoing principals of this period were heroes, villains, or simply pawns of the larger circumstance, as are we all, to varying degrees."[139] Memories of Prohibition tend to romanticize the adventurers. Frank Butler, Bill McCoy, and many more became wealthy during Prohibition; countless others suffered recriminations and poverty in this era.

One rumrunner expressed the opinion of many: "I don't want to remember; I want to forget."

Kingsbury was a teenager growing up in the era of Prohibition. His recollections were those of a wide-eyed naïf. "It was god-damned lively here during Prohibition....This was a way station (for rum-runners) and we also had a lot of geniuses here cooking up their own bug juice."

He went on: "Making moonshine was a cottage industry on the Island.... One old guy peddled moonshine out of a baby carriage. My aunt used to say, 'That lovely little man, he's always wheeling his little child along the street.' Silk Stocking Sam, he was called."

Vineyarders had their own means of dealing with Prohibition. "The old-time Portuguese were well into wine-making, also brandy." And "The Tiltons used to bring in Belgian alcohol aboard their coaster." Kingsbury claimed that one day whaleman George Fred Tilton asked him to help lug four-gallon cans of Belgian alcohol from Church's pier in Oak Bluffs harbor up Circuit Avenue to the Pawnee House. In public. Kingsbury explained, "All the hotels sold booze to their guests. They wouldn't buy the local moonshine but wanted the good stuff." As someone who knew, or sounded like he knew, he said, "There was no problem getting a drink during Prohibition."[140]

Linsey Lee compiled quotes from Vineyarders on their recollections of Prohibition:

> "And if they were being chased, or if they thought they were going to be chased, they'd dump it [the liquor], and come back and get it."
>
> —Gale Huntington (1902–1993), Vineyard Haven

> "The Coast Guard boats were out in the shoals, and most of the time Frank Butler would slip by them. And then, of course, when they were shooting, if that boat was out here and they had to shoot toward land, they couldn't shoot. So Butler knew the water good enough, he just skimmed the rocks here. I never heard of him going up on the rocks."
>
> —Charles Vanderhoop (1921–2001), Aquinnah

> "I knew there was one [bootleg still] down at the corner of County Road and Barnes Road [in Oak Bluffs]. The fellow that manufactured stuff, his nickname was 'Half Pint.'"
>
> —Elisha Smith (1923–2013), Vineyard Haven

In 2022...

With the legalization of marijuana in Massachusetts, it's now possible to step into a "traditional apothecary," Fine Fettle Dispensary, in West Tisbury, that features medicinal and adult-use recreational marijuana. In Vineyard Haven, Island Time offers the product, locally grown.

17
SCOPES

The Scopes Trial of 1925 was a cultural conflict between religion and science. Scopes was an attempt by fundamentalists to attack modernists on the teaching of evolution in state-funded public schools. It took place in an atmosphere of intense political challenges to science. The Scopes Trial drew national headlines in a contrived controversy between religion and science, between the past and the present.

News reports of the trial circulated across the country in mid-July 1925. John Scopes was a Tennessee high school teacher accused of violating the Butler Act, which forbade teaching human evolution. William Jennings Bryan, who had run for and lost a bid for president three times, served as attorney for the prosecution. His argument was that the study of evolution was contrary to the Bible; the word of God preempted the scientific facts of evolution that Scopes sought to teach. Defense Attorney Clarence Darrow supported Scopes, arguing that human evolution did not contradict religious beliefs; both science and religion could function in society.

Bryan won the case, which affirmed that the word of God preempted the scientific study of evolution. Scopes was found guilty and fined one hundred dollars; however, the case was overturned on a technicality, so he did not pay the fine.

In the 1920s, there were movements to explore and expose historical events, to explain and expand their importance or justify their actions or reactions. Nothing was as dramatic as the Scopes Trial, but Martha's Vineyard enjoyed a couple of cases of historical revisionism in the 1920s.

This story was first published in the *Vineyard Gazette* in 1854. A fugitive slave had been rescued by the Underground Railroad on Martha's Vineyard and sent on to freedom in Canada.

In the original report, Captain Cook of the bark *Franklin* from Jacksonville, Florida, put in at Holmes Hole Harbor, unaware he had a stowaway. The fugitive slave's name was Randall Burton, and he escaped from the ship, making off in a small boat. Captain Cook notified authorities, as the law required, and waited, at anchor, for the escapee to be recaptured so he could be returned to Florida. The delay in tracking down the fugitive aided his escape.

Initially, Burton had been assisted by stevedores in Florida who hid him aboard the *Franklin*. It was later learned he also had contacts in Kennebec, Maine, awaiting his arrival, but he had already skipped out on Martha's Vineyard. Randall Burton was thirty-one, born in Williamston, North Carolina, and was anxious to make his way to freedom in the North.

The *Gazette* reported the fugitive had taken a boat to West Chop, then made his way to Gay Head, where he hid in a swamp. Two women from Holmes Hole determined to help Burton. They brought food and clothing in a cart out to Gay Head, where they met Burton by the swamp. The women persuaded him to don a disguise of female apparel. Together they rode in the cart to Menemsha and arranged a small boat to take the three of them across Buzzard's Bay to New Bedford. There the two unnamed women met with an abolitionist who arranged to transfer Randall Burton to freedom in Canada.

No mention was made of either the potential danger of aiding an escaped slave or the potential $1,000 fine to the women had they been accosted by Sheriff Lambert, whose pursuit of Burton was underway. That is the sum and substance of the original story, published in 1854.

Now for the rest of the story, the revised version of a historical incident.

On February 3, 1921, the *Vineyard Gazette* published an article by Netta Vanderhoop titled "The True Story of a Fugitive Slave." The original story, in 1854, was "A Runaway Slave."

According to Netta, her grandmother Beulah Vanderhoop was involved in the original rescue back in 1854. Netta corroborated the original story but made it clear it was her grandmother, a Wampanoag woman, and not the two (white) women from Holmes Hole who rescued the escapee. Netta wrote her letter to correct and emphasize the role her Wampanoag ancestor played in assisting escaped slaves years ago.

It is still a dramatic story. However, the revised version stands as a testament to the bravery and collaboration of the Wampanoag in the era of the Fugitive Slave Act.

Netta Vanderhoop changed a few facts in the original story. She stated the ship was from Charleston, South Carolina, rather than Jacksonville, Florida. She thought the captain put in at Holmes Hole rather than continue to Boston; the original version had the ship going on to Kennebec, Maine.

Netta acknowledged the dangers her grandmother accepted in assisting the runaway. "The laws of those days were so rigid that men generally neither dared nor cared to assist escaping slaves."

In the 1921 version of the escape, Netta changed the fugitive's name to Edgar Jones and stated he managed to get ashore. He survived "for three days, [and] he hid in the woods and cornfields, living on raw corn." She did not explain how he made his way to Gay Head, but once there, Jones stayed for a week with a local Wampanoag, Moses Bassett, who offered Edgar Jones food and lodging in return for work. This was not only helping an escaped slave but also hiring a laborer who needed food and shelter in return for his work.

Soon, the sheriff learned of the fugitive in Gay Head and set out after him.

Netta Vanderhoop described her version of the encounter. Edgar Jones escaped from Bassett's farm ahead of the sheriff and found refuge in the home of Postmaster William Vanderhoop and his wife, Beulah, who was Netta's grandmother. Beulah recognized the seriousness of the situation: Edgar Jones was a fugitive. The sheriff was after him. Jones needed to be rescued. Beulah pulled out some old clothes and convinced Jones to don them, disguised as a woman. "The fugitive obeyed the kindest mistress he had ever had and step by step approached his freedom."[141]

The Wampanoag of Gay Head supported the Underground Railroad. Samuel Peters offered to sail Jones across Vineyard Sound to New Bedford, "for the people of Gay Head knew that if he once reached there, he would be perfectly safe." The two brave men, one a Native American, the other a Black man, sailed across the Sound and reached the Quaker city by seven o'clock the next morning. Edgar Jones stepped ashore to freedom.

Netta's letter states that Jones worked as a free man on the wharves of New Bedford for several years and kept in touch with the Vanderhoops. Shortly before the Civil War, Jones left New Bedford, headed for San Francisco.

It is intriguing to postulate why Netta Vanderhoop felt moved to document her grandmother's brave exploits. Obviously, she was proud of her grandmother's role in the rescue. That her story so closely parallels the published piece from 1854 indicates she was intent on reinforcing the original story yet wanted to make sure her grandmother got credit.

Interestingly, Netta's grandson Captain Charles Vanderhoop Jr. repeated the escape tale in his interview with Linsey Lee in 2000. He added this intriguing line to Netta's story: "I think it was a total of eight slaves that she saved."[142]

Repetition of family lore recalls Wampanoag storytelling accounts of tribal life, passed down the decades, through the generations, repeating and retelling old tales to keep the story alive for the current and future members of the tribe. This is an intriguing exercise. Not only does it serve as a recounting of the history of our forebears, but it is also a worthy recognition of a noble event. And it serves to correct or rewrite and reinforce history.

The statue of a Union soldier stands proudly on the corner of Ocean Park in Oak Bluffs. It was originally installed at the foot of Circuit Avenue, Farland Square (formerly Monument Square), in 1891 by Charles Strahan, editor of the *Martha's Vineyard Herald*, formerly the *Cottage City Star*.

Strahan was a Confederate soldier from Maryland who fought in the Civil War.

Editor Strahan purchased the statue from the J.W. Fiske Company of New York. Identical statues stand in front of the town hall in North Kingstown, Rhode Island, in Illinois, and New Jersey. Strahan paid for the statue through newspaper subscriptions. His intent was to heal the wounds that lingered from the Civil War among Union soldiers, represented by their local veterans' organization, the Grand Army of the Republic (GAR).

When the statue was first dedicated in August 1891, Strahan was quoted as saying, "That this comes from one who once wore gray, I trust will add significance to the fact that we are once more a union of Americans. A union which endears with equal honor the citizen of Georgia with the citizen of Maine; that Massachusetts and South Carolina are again

The soldier statue in Oak Bluffs was painted gray in the 1980s, which prompted some people to think he represented a Confederate soldier. Not so. *Photo by Joyce Dresser.*

brothers; that there is no North nor South, no East nor West, but one undivided, indivisible union."

While the statue was a symbolic effort to heal the wounds of war, Strahan always sought to do more, to heal the rift that continued to linger between North and South. As a southerner who lived and worked in New England, he recognized and valued the importance of the Union. Strahan sought to soothe the souls of the Vineyard veterans, invoking the public to share in his effort.

Born in 1839, Strahan enlisted in Company B of the Maryland Guards at Richmond, Virginia, attached to the Twenty-First Virginia Infantry. He was wounded in the Battle of Gettysburg in 1863. After the war, he worked at Levering, Strahan and Company, importing coffee from New Orleans. In 1884, he moved to Martha's Vineyard.

In 1891, Strahan's five-year-old daughter unveiled the soldier statue by the Strand Theatre. Strahan said it was his wish that "the sons of the gray will stand with the sons of the blue, should any foe, domestic or foreign, dare attack that flag." Strahan anticipated that "the day might soon come when the name of a Confederate soldier might be placed on a face of the monument which he had left blank for that purpose."

By 1925, decades later, Charles Strahan again wanted to set the record straight from his perspective. As a former Confederate soldier, he had come to recognize that the Union was more important than the sectional divide brought on by states' rights' support of slavery. Strahan lived to see his wish fulfilled. He was present when the statue was rededicated and a fourth plaque added to the base of the statue.

The *Gazette* noted in 1925 that "few young people know that this soldier is still living, at 86 years of age who bears the scars of Yankee bullets to this day. Lieut. Strahan is apparently as vigorous as many men of 50. Quick of movement, erect of carriage and with his closely trimmed beard and mustache as white as snow, he is every inch the retired army officer."[143]

The fourth plaque on the statue was installed at the ceremony. It read, "The chasm is closed. In memory of the restored Union this tablet is dedicated by Union veterans of the Civil War and patriotic citizens of Martha's Vineyard in honor of the Confederate soldiers."[144]

The plaque remained secured to the statue's base for nearly a century.

Initially, the statue was known as the Soldiers' Memorial Fountain. The trough in the plinth served as a watering station for passing horses, the primary means of transport in 1891. By 1930, however, a new mode of transport, the automobile, had flooded the Island, and the statue was removed from Circuit Avenue to make way for a traffic light. Unfortunately, shortly after it was moved, the iconic statue fell off its base, damaging limb and weapon.

Seven decades later, repairs were made to the statue, orchestrated by David Wilson of Oak Bluffs. Wilson had necessary parts molded from the sister statue in Rhode Island. The new location, on the edge of Ocean Park, now greets tourists stepping or driving off the steamship. Picnic tables invite visitors to share time or sustenance in the shadow of the stately statue.

As historian Matthew Stackpole said at the re-dedication in 2001, "History isn't important if it is something you just look back at. History is only important if it applies to today and tomorrow. This statue is a way to remember our history and move ahead."[145]

Stackpole's words resonated following the controversial right-wing Nazi march in 2017 in Charlottesville, Virginia. Civil War statues were removed across the country as they honored the Confederacy. To that end, an effort was made in Oak Bluffs to remove the statue in 2019 because the 1925 plaque honored soldiers of the Confederacy that seceded from the Union in 1861.

"The issue emerged at a Board of Selectmen meeting in March [2019] when NAACP supporters demanded the plaques be removed while local veterans asked that the plaques stay put."[146]

The outcome of the selectmen's meeting was to remove the offending plaques and house them at the Martha's Vineyard Museum. The plaques now (2022) hang in Doherty Hall, with appropriate descriptions of the historical controversy hopefully set right.

History has been reviewed and revised in the story of the Soldiers' Memorial in Oak Bluffs. The facts are what they are. How we honor or recognize the past may change over time, but the facts cannot, and should not, be ignored or denied.

One summer, Joan Woollcott, one of the four Woollcott sisters of West Chop and Baltimore, got a summer job working for the *Gazette*. Her assignment was to interview people about their pets. At first, she was inspired to report on the hijinks of puppies and cats, but her interest waned when one woman said she spanked her goldfish when they were naughty. (We were unable to ascertain the date this occurred but confirmed Joan Woollcott worked for the *Vineyard Gazette*.)

The Woollcott sisters were pet lovers themselves. Their mother, however, was more responsible for providing care and comfort of their four-legged cohabitants. Joan took it on herself to write a piece for the paper on how her mother showed more interest in the family dog Chico than in her four daughters. She bragged to her family how she wrote, "Mother fussed over the dog, how she treated him like a very superior human being, and how she actually seemed to prefer him to her children." When the Tuesday summer edition of the paper came out, Joan was thrilled.[147]

On Friday, Joan picked up the latest edition of the *Gazette*.

"There, placed prominently on the editorial page, was a letter which the Houghs had printed without Joan's knowledge." Joan was taken aback by the letter, which read in part, "When I speak to Chico, he listens attentively, and tries his best to obey me. My children never listen at all.…When I come into a room, Chico rises politely. My children give no indication that they are aware of my presence." The letter was signed, Marie Woollcott.

History can and should be understood; it can be acknowledged by individuals in a different way, but the facts, the truth, must always be recognized.

IN 1920...

"Legislatures in twenty states, most of them in the South, considered thirty-seven anti-evolution measures."[148]

18

END OF AN ERA

On the day the stock market fell, precipitating the Great Depression, the *Vineyard Gazette* published a piece titled "King's Highway Is Known Only to Few."

King's Highway runs through Chilmark, parallel to and halfway between South and Middle Roads. Today it is accessible just south of Abel's Hill and is noted on several hiking maps. Yet in 1929, the *Gazette* challenged its readers: "Not many Vineyarders have heard of the 'King's Highway' or know that any such road exists on the Island."[149]

King's Highway originally ran from the West Tisbury–Chilmark town line south to Beetlebung Corner. It was the old road from West Tisbury out to Quitsa, by Squibnocket Beach. In 1929, it was only a walking trail, and the *Gazette* cautioned, "It would hardly be advisable to attempt to drive through it with a valuable new vehicle because of the growth of underbrush and overhanging tree limbs."

"King's Highway passes through a veritable network of ancient roads," the article continued and postulated that it was laid out as late as 1704. More than likely the King's Highway was "the original South Road and the first public highway in the town, probably the only one previous to the Revolution." It could have been the first "hie way" in the town.

And that was the day the stock market collapsed, Tuesday, October 25, 1929.

King's Highway winds through Chilmark, from West Tisbury to Squibnocket. *Photo by Joyce Dresser.*

First announced in the midwinter of 1928, the vast sum of $35 million seemed too good to be true. And it was. The story was teased along for a couple of weeks in the *Gazette*: thirty-five generous citizens were donating $35 million to Martha's Vineyard. As the story grew, so too did the fund. Two more donors joined, and the number soared to $37 million. What was this all about?

The *Vineyard Gazette* offered its readers the chance to suggest how to spend the money. Most people could spend only a couple of million, but the more imaginative offered impressive suggestions: dredge Edgartown and Vineyard Haven Harbors; build a new school in Vineyard Haven; design a park for Gay Head; pave more streets in Oak Bluffs.

Once ideas began to circulate, the *Gazette* acknowledged that the fund was only in its first stage. The $37 million was essentially the interest that would be earned over the course of the next three centuries. The thirty-seven donors had each contributed $10 to an account at the Edgartown National Bank. At 4 percent annual interest, such a fund would make a millionaire out of the twelfth-generation grandchild of each donor, paying out $1,013,175 on the first of March 2219. What could be wrong with that?

This novel approach to savings was first proposed by Benjamin Franklin in 1789. "Franklin stands out as one of the great men of all history. In science, government, literature, philosophy, education and a hundred practical arts he made surprising contributions."[150] Franklin set up two funds with £1,000 each, one in Boston, another in Philadelphia. The funds were to be held for a century, with money doled out to deserving young business entrepreneurs and for municipal improvements in the community. Boston's Franklin Park and Franklin Institute benefited from the Franklin Fund; eighty-five thousand Boston students received monies over the years.

After a century of compounded interest, in 1890, Franklin's great-grandchildren sought access to the funds but were denied by courts in both

Philadelphia and Boston. City officials in Philadelphia used the interest for an inordinate amount for questionable purposes, leaving their fund with $100,000 in 1890, while Boston had some $430,000. A century later, in 1990, when the accounts were closed, Philadelphia had $2 million and Boston $4.5 million. Once those two accounts were closed, the money was distributed to colleges and programs previously established by the Franklin Fund.

Benjamin Franklin's initial deposit turned into a pot of gold two centuries down the road, a generous gift from the past to the present. Pay it forward, as they say.

In the 1920s, six cities across the country established similar funds. Based on population, the Vineyard Trust would return a greater amount per capita than any of the six cities already saving for their future: Portland, Oregon; Muncie, Indiana; Meriden and New London, Connecticut; New Bedford and Lawrence, Massachusetts.

The $37 million would be available in 2219, a mere 291 years to wait for the bounty. In the meantime, the *Gazette* offered $50 to letter writers who offered the best suggestions on how to spend the money. "These discussions, however, turned the public attention to the needs of the Vineyard, and during the last two weeks hundreds of imaginary public buildings have been erected, schools and historical societies have been endowed, harbors have been improved, and new boat lines established."[151]

"One generation hence the Vineyard's fund will have grown to significant proportions and it is easy to imagine the interest and even the awe of the Island's children and children's children as the dollars accumulate like a snowball increasing in size, growing and rolling on to fulfill its mission in the Vineyard's destiny."[152]

Thinking of the future makes us consider the present, the needs we can attain right now. We could provide housing for people in need; rebuild the Tisbury school and the high school; build bike paths on Beach Road in Vineyard Haven and Up-Island; and expand parks and conservation sites across the Island. It's fun to dream.

Twenty months after the excitement generated by the Vineyard Trust and nearly a month after the stock market crash of 1929, the *Gazette* offered a few words, a very few words, of reaction to the plummeting financial markets.

"To what extent the Island's business will be affected by the crash of the stock market has been a question uppermost in many minds." Calmly, editor Hough sought to ease the crisis with passive commentary. "As to the Vineyard itself, there has been and is no panic."[153] Of course, at the time, no one could foresee how devastating, complex, and complete the Great Depression would become. In any case, the *Gazette* offered a reserved approach to the crisis. The Island still welcomed tourists and visitors, expanding the horizon wherever possible.

Dorothy West offered her perspective on the Depression as it hit the Island: "Then it was 1929, and the stock market crash, and on its heels, the Depression. And for the decade following the crash, Oak Bluffs suffered a lingering sickness of meagre summers. It was the town hardest hit because it was the town whose summer business had been its only business."[154]

Crash: A History of the Great Depression and the Fall and Rise of America is a book compiled by West Tisbury resident Marc Favreau for young adults. The book offers a vivid account of the Depression with plenty of explanatory detail. It shows how the American people were devastated but survived and moved on.

"It started because I'm obsessed with this collection of photographs at the Library of Congress," Favreau said. "I thought I would take a collection of those and tell the story of the Great Depression with photographs and minor captions that were strung together. That evolved into a book."[155]

At the beginning, Favreau writes, "America did not see it coming. In 1929, the United States was riding high on a great bubble of energy and excitement sometimes called the 'Roaring Twenties.' Radios blared music in living rooms and dance halls, champagne and gin—both illegal—flowed freely in 'speakeasy' clubs; young men and women everywhere practiced the newest dance steps late into the evenings."

Nearly two years after the market collapsed, the *Vineyard Gazette* blindly ignored the increasingly dire economic situation. An editorial published on June 16, 1931, blandly suggested, "Sea bathing is said to be the best cure for Depression."

As if people had not lost their bank accounts, their jobs, or their homes, Hough blithely noted, "All along the Island waterfront summer craft have suddenly appeared like waterfowl which have just finished hibernating." The *Gazette* pretended this was just a typical summer.

And stubbornly, the *Gazette* admonished its readers, "There should be a limit to all this popular worry about the depression; the depression which is, incidentally, about over. If it were not for worry, we can see no reason why almost anyone should not come to Martha's Vineyard this summer and have a splendid time."

Hough concluded, wistfully, "Depressions may come and go, but normal living requires that vacations should continue without change; Vineyard vacations, with sea air and sun and unspoiled landscapes among which to play and rest." And that was 1931, as the Depression was just heating up.

Favreau described stark facts about the Depression in *Crash*. Black Tuesday occurred on Tuesday, October 29, 1929, when stockbrokers sold their certificates and the market collapsed. People lost their savings, their retirement, their future. Within six months, a quarter of all workers were unemployed. A third of all banks closed, beginning in November 1930.

The Bonus Army, twenty-three thousand veterans, camped out in Washington, D.C., seeking benefits promised after the First World War. General Douglas MacArthur disrupted their encampment on July 28, 1932, in a public-relations fiasco. President Herbert Hoover was vilified for his treatment of veterans. Across the country, Hoover flags (empty pockets), Hoover blankets (newspapers), and Hoovervilles (homeless shanties) proliferated.

In the election of November 1932, Franklin Delano Roosevelt received 23 million votes, the most ever for a presidential candidate up to that time. In his inaugural address on March 4, 1933, FDR said, "So first of all let me assert my firm belief that the only thing we have to fear is fear itself—nameless, unreasoning, unjustified terror which paralyzes needed efforts to convert retreat into advance." That dramatic phrase signaled that FDR recognized the depths of economic disaster facing the country and was poised to address the concerns and fears of the citizenry.

Sixty million people tuned in to FDR's first fireside chat on March 12, 1933, when he addressed the banking crisis, the stock market situation, and the slowdown of the economy.

"As president and First Lady, Franklin and Eleanor Roosevelt were not only husband and wife, but also each other's closest confidant and most reliable political ally. Like Franklin, Eleanor kept up a gigantic network of friends, supporters, readers, and informal advisors."[156]

Favreau continued: "Above all, she helped mobilize those people who had previously found themselves excluded from American politics—especially women—and made sure the White House stayed sympathetic to their needs and hopes."

When FDR was inaugurated, manufacturing had shut down and the automobile business was functioning at 20 percent capacity. A quarter million families faced eviction, and two million homeless people wandered from street to street, town to town; teenagers made up half a million of this homeless cohort. Fifteen million people were searching for work.

"The Great Depression didn't just destroy jobs and savings (to the point that an estimated 28 per cent of the population had no income), it damaged people's souls."[157]

Franklin Roosevelt's New Deal brought the country out of the Great Depression. The focus had to change dramatically from individual investment to the federal government actively assisting citizens to get back on their feet, find a job, a home, and a future.

Op-editor Gregory Wallace noted, "On the Vineyard, up-Islanders, in particular, actually fended better for themselves because, according to one oral history, they could hunt, fish, and farm."[158]

And on Island, the Edgartown swordfishing business remained strong. Fancy restaurants in Boston served the fish, increasingly popular with those who still had funds to dine out. "Five or six schooners from Edgartown would go out for a couple of weeks and return with a 'cash crop' in their holds. After selling their catch in Boston, they would sail into Edgartown for a few days at home, their crews with fat rolls of bills in their pockets. It was a good time to be a swordfisherman, but little else."[159]

Oak Bluffs was hard hit, although many hotels were still able to remain open each summer. Dorothy West recalled Oak Bluffs during the Depression: "The great houses stood empty, too large to run without servants, and too few, if any, families who could still afford a staff. The hotels and shops that struggled to stay open were barely staying alive. 'For Sale' signs were everywhere, and there were no buyers."[160] It was a desolate time to be sure.

Carpenters and painters struggled to find work. Tourism was weak. Building virtually stopped on the Vineyard during the Depression. Optimistically, Henry Beetle Hough suggested in his *Gazette* editorial of June 16, 1931, that "a vacation here is not an extravagance." He went on: "So far there has been no overproduction of sea air and no collapse of the market in green hills and sandy beaches."

And he facetiously promised, "The things for which money is paid on the Island are the less essential things, such as food, clothing and shelter. Our real luxuries are free for the taking, as every bather and picnicker should know."

Most people in the 1920s were unaware of the partridge-like heath hen. Its population had been decimated over the years, a far cry from the mid-nineteenth century when servants requested not to have to eat heath hen more than twice a week because it was so populous and easy to capture.

By the start of the twentieth century, the heath hen had become extinct everywhere except on Martha's Vineyard. Hence, in 1908, the Massachusetts legislature established six hundred acres for the State Forest, "for the purpose of establishing on the tract a state reservation for the better protection of the heath hen, or pinnated

The last heath hen represented the end of an era, the symbol of extinction. *Courtesy of the* Vineyard Gazette.

grouse. As is well known," it was reported, "the few fowl of this species on the Vineyard are the last of this famous branch of the grouse family. Nowhere else in the world are these heath hens found."[161]

Unfortunately, the heath hen preferred low brush and bushes to trees, so the forest became an anomaly for the bird. Heath hen numbers were further decimated by forest fires.

The last remaining heath hen, Booming Ben, the most famous resident of Martha's Vineyard, still made his rounds in 1927, avoiding hunters and errant motorists. The president of the Massachusetts Fish and Game Association almost ran over the iconic bird while motoring along the Dr. Fisher Road in West Tisbury. This last extant heath hen was seen on March 11, 1932, and is now extinct.

It was reported in the early months of the New Deal that "a conservation army, numbering 219 men, will arrive on the Island today to take up the work of reforestation in the state reservation under the federal plan for relieving unemployment."[162]

Mosher Photo enjoyed an unintended consequence from these off-Islanders arriving for work with the Civilian Conservation Corps. They lived in a work camp in the State Forest. The young men of the CCC were paid $30 per month, of which $25 was sent home to their families. These men created fire lanes crisscrossing the State Forest, trimmed trees, and removed brush. The off-Islanders were so impressed by the natural beauty of the Vineyard that they took dozens of photographs of the landscape. Mosher Photo, which opened its doors in 1923 and closed them in 2021, became a success story by developing the film so the young men could send photos back home to friends and family.

The Cape Cod Canal was dug in the early 1920s. It initially operated as a private waterway, charging tolls. Yet the canal was too narrow and too shallow for large vessels. The federal government bought the canal in 1928 but did nothing with it until the Depression.

The Works Progress Administration brought 1,400 unemployed men to the Cape. Men from the WPA widened and deepened the canal, rebuilding it to 500 feet wide and 32 feet deep. Two bridges were built across the waterway, the Sagamore and the Bourne. At the time, it was deemed the largest sea-level canal in the world; no locks were needed. The Cape Cod Canal was reopened in 1940, and life on the Cape has never been the same. This proved a major boon for the shipping industry but hurt Vineyard Haven, which had been a welcome harbor along the East Coast route for centuries.

"Somehow, even at the bottom of the depression, Oak Bluffs managed to stay alive. Guests still came to the big old hotels, still sat on their porches, rocking the hours away, entertained by the evening flow of vacationers and Islanders along the avenue. It was a joy for all who could afford to come."[163] Homemade ice cream was still served at Rausch's; a nickel bag of popcorn awaited at Darlings. Circuit Avenue was alive then, as it is today.

In 2020...
We still have several years left to savor the decade of the 2020s. Who knows what will happen? We look for peace, love, economic stability, and expanded civil rights across the Island and around the world. Each of us has a role to play in making those dreams a reality.

EPILOGUE

And so, we leave the Roaring Twenties and pull ourselves back into the present, dealing once again with a pandemic, a war in Europe, restrictions on immigration, and fears of the spread of Communism. Voting rights are an issue today, as they were a century ago. Prohibition of illicit drugs replaces prohibition on selling alcohol.

Today, African and Native Americans and immigrants try to exert more influence on the community, just as they did in the 1920s. Today the internet dominates the *Vineyard Gazette* and the radio as the primary means of communication. The automobile still rules the roads, as it did a century ago when it pushed aside the trolley.

People liked to party in the 1920s, dancing at the Tivoli or sipping illicit liquor. A century ago, young women who went out dancing, drinking, driving, and smoking were known as flappers. Today, unconventional attire and activity have become conventional.

During the 1920s, the Vineyard established itself as a resort community. Today, that image has become the standard of Island life, dominating our economy, affecting our lifestyle. During the 1920s, no one imagined the bottom would fall out of a prosperity that knew no limits. And yet, when the Depression hit at the end of the decade, Vineyarders managed to eke out a living, fishing, catering to those vacationers who still had money, and finding odd jobs to make ends meet.

Throughout the decade of the 1920s, the country experienced a cultural shift as some freedoms were expanded, such as suffrage and fashion, while others were curtailed: think Prohibition and immigration. Public education survived the impact of the Scopes Trial. The Red Scare bloomed and faded for a time.

Money was made hand-over-fist in the financial capital of the country. The wealth of the United States doubled in the 1920s. Martha's Vineyard grew in popularity as more visitors, summer people, and tourists discovered the Island, and it continued to expand into a summer resort.

As we look ahead, none of us know whether we will face another financial panic, another pandemic, or a climatic crisis beyond our wildest fears. Or perhaps we will be the beneficiaries of an unimagined proverbial blessing of a restoration of a stable climate, an unexpected economic windfall, or the elevation of a peaceful world order.

It's often been said that those who fail to learn from history are destined to repeat it. Let us trust that the 1920s have taught us something about learning to live in a more realistic, optimistic world.

NOTES

Prologue

1. West, *The Richer, The Poorer*, 239.

1. War

2. Myrick, "Sons of Gay Head Stood Strong."
3. *Vineyard Gazette*, July 18, 1918.
4. Dresser, *Hidden History*, 64.

2. Pandemic

5. *Vineyard Gazette*, October 3, 1918.
6. *MV Magazine*, November 1, 2018, from *Vineyard Gazette*, December 17, 1918.

3. Prohibition I

7. Railton, "Story of Martha's Vineyard."
8. Currier, "Let's Raise a Glass."
9. Ibid.
10. Allen, *Black Ships*, 4.
11. *Vineyard Gazette*, August 4, 1921.
12. Scoville, *Shipwrecks on Martha's Vineyard*, 38.
13. Ibid.; Allen, *Black Ships*, 30.

14. Currier, "Let's Raise a Glass."
15. Wood and Wood, *Nomans Land*, preface.
16. Ibid., 107.
17. Ibid.; Allen, *Black Ships*, 196.
18. Allen, *Black Ships*, 201.
19. *Vineyard Gazette*, August 12, 1923.
20. Ibid.; Allen, *Black Ships*, 205.
21. Baer, "This Was Then."
22. Ibid.; Wood and Wood, *Nomans Land*, 108.

4. Suffrage

23. *Vineyard Gazette*, September 9, 1920.
24. Ibid.
25. *Vineyard Gazette*, 1932.
26. *Vineyard Gazette*, August 11, 1921.
27. Brewster and Huey-Burns, "Proposals to Restrict Voting Gain Traction."

5. Fashion

28. Joan Boyken, email, March 4, 2022.

6. Music

29. Dresser, *Music of Martha's Vineyard*, 33.
30. Ibid.; West, *The Richer, The Poorer*, 175.
31. Dresser, *Music on Martha's Vineyard*, 29.
32. Ibid.
33. Railton, *History of Martha's Vineyard*, 353.
34. Macmackin, "From the Tivoli to the Ocean View."
35. Ibid.; Dresser, *Music on Martha's Vineyard*, 32.
36. Ibid.
37. Dresser, *Music on Martha's Vineyard*, 32.
38. Ibid., 39.
39. Richter, *Fiddles, Harmonicas and Banjos*, 47. Her 2008 thesis first divined Benton's musical explorations.
40. Dresser, *Music on Martha's Vineyard*, 40.
41. Ibid.; Richter, *Fiddles, Harmonicas and Banjos*, 40.
42. Dresser, *Music on Martha's Vineyard*, 40.
43. Richter, *Fiddles, Harmonicas and Banjos*, 39.

44. Williamson, "Singing 1920s."
45. IMDb, "Annabelle Lee: User Reviews," https://www.imdb.com/title/tt0011925/, December 13, 2012.
46. Robards, "'Annabell Lee' Shows Menemsha."
47. Dunlop, "Historic Film Clips Reveal Edgartown," https://vineyardgazette.com/news/2016/05/26/historic-film-clips-reveal-edgartown-1925.
48. Ibid.
49. *Vineyard Gazette*, "About Historic Movies on Martha's Vineyard," https://vineyardgazette.com/about-historic-movies-marthas-vineyard.
50. Wallcox, "Snowbirds."
51. Ibid.

7. Immigration

52. *Vineyard Gazette*, September 9, 1929.
53. *Vineyard Gazette*, June 24, 1930.
54. Ibid.
55. Baer, "Islands to Island."
56. Baer, "Immigrants."
57. Dresser, *Women of Martha's Vineyard*, 107.
58. Berry, "Have Faith."
59. Ibid.; Baer, "Islands to Island."

8. Migration

60. History.com, "Great Migration," https://www.history.com/topics/black-history/great-migration.
61. Remastered in Kind, "How Did the Harlem Renaissance Start?" https://remasteredinkind.com/how-did-the-harlem-renaissance-start/.
62. Ibid.
63. Cromwell, "History of Oak Bluffs."
64. Wallcox, "February 13, 1913."
65. *Vineyard Gazette*, September 2, 1927.
66. Railton, "Story of Martha's Vineyard."

9. Renaissance

67. Ibid.; Cromwell, "History of Oak Bluffs," 15.
68. Christiansen, "Shearer Family."
69. Dresser, *Tourism on Martha's Vineyard*, 111.

70. Ibid.; Cromwell, "History of Oak Bluffs," 15.
71. West, *The Richer, The Poorer*, 179.
72. It is worth noting that Abigail McGrath, who is Helene Johnson's daughter and Dorothy West's niece, operates a writers' retreat in Oak Bluffs, appropriately named Renaissance House. McGrath organizes the annual public recitation of Frederick Douglass's 1852 speech "What to the Slave Is the Fourth of July?" and contributes to the *Martha's Vineyard Times*.
73. West, *The Richer, The Poorer*, 215.
74. Black Nerd News, "Dorothy West," https://blacknerdnews.com/dorothy-west/.
75. Railton, *History of Martha's Vineyard*, 94.
76. Lee, *Vineyard Voices*, 35.

10. Barn House

77. Railton, "Story of Martha's Vineyard."
78. Ibid.
79. Ibid.
80. Road Trippers, "Barn House, Chilmark," https://maps.roadtrippers.com/us/chilmark-ma/points-of-interest/barn-house-chilmark-ma.
81. Railton, "Story of Martha's Vineyard."
82. History.com Editors, "Red Scare," February 28, 2020, https://www.history.com/topics/cold-war/red-scare.
83. Railton, "Story of Martha's Vineyard."
84. Ibid.

11. Radicals

85. Railton, "Tom Benton."
86. Ibid.
87. Herman, "Crystal Eastman,"
88. Scutts, "How Crystal Eastman Fought."
89. Ibid.
90. Herman, "Crystal Eastman,"
91. Railton, "Tom Benton."
92. Irmscher, *Max Eastman*, 291.
93. Ibid.
94. Trotter, "IU's Eastman Residency."
95. *Vineyard Gazette*, 1969.

12. History

96. *Vineyard Gazette*, October 30, 1925.
97. Lee, *Vineyard Voices Three*, 188.
98. Hufstader, "Still Learning."
99. Wilson, "Information, Improvement, Sociability."
100. *Vineyard Gazette*, October 5, 1928.

13. Business

101. Kolleth, "Name Phillips Means Hardware."
102. Shea, "Phillips Hardware."
103. Hufstader, "Cronig's Celebrates 100 Years."
104. Baer, "Immigrants."
105. *Vineyard Gazette*, June 15, 1922.
106. *Vineyard Gazette*, November 2, 1928.
107. *Vineyard Gazette*, July 8, 1930.
108. Ibid.
109. *Vineyard Gazette*, May 25, 1928.
110. *Vineyard Gazette*, October 5, 1928.
111. Ibid.; Meras, *Country Editor*, 62.

14. Transport

112. Martha's Vineyard Commission, "Martha's Vineyard Statistical Profile, February 2019," https://www.mvcommission.org/sites/default/files/docs/web01_MVSP%20FINAL%20PRINT%202019-03-21-3.pdf.
113. *Vineyard Gazette*, July 31, 1919.
114. Railton, "Story of Martha's Vineyard."
115. "Seagrave, State Study Details Drawbacks to Alternate Freight Port," *Vineyard Gazette*, February 17, 2022.

15. Wrecks

116. *Vineyard Gazette*, April 12, 1923.
117. *Vineyard Gazette*, July 3, 1924.
118. Ibid.
119. Mass.gov, "Kershaw," https://www.mass.gov.
120. Ibid.
121. *New York Times*, June 2, 1928.

122. Mass.gov, "Kershaw."
123. Ibid.
124. *Vineyard Gazette*, June 8, 1928.

16. Prohibition II

125. Wood and Wood, *Nomans Land*, 109.
126. Allen, *Black Ships*, 214.
127. Ibid.
128. Ibid., preface, xi.
129. Ibid., 146.
130. Baer, "This Was Then."
131. Allen, *Black Ships*, 147.
132. Ibid., 182.
133. Ibid., 185.
134. Ibid., 188.
135. Currier, "Let's Raise a Glass."
136. Allen, *Black Ships*, 278.
137. Ibid.
138. Currier, "Let's Raise a Glass."
139. Allen, *Black Ships*, 285.
140. Railton, "Craig Kingsbury."

17. Scopes

141. *Vineyard Gazette*, February 3, 1921.
142. Lee, *More Vineyard Voices*, 114.
143. *Vineyard Gazette*, June 5, 1925.
144. "Monument to Healing," *Vineyard Gazette*, August 17, 2017, https://vineyardgazette.com/news/2017/08/17/monument-healing.
145. "Oak Bluffs Civil War Statue Rededicated," *Vineyard Gazette*, August 20, 2001.
146. "Civil War Statue Reopens Old Wounds," *Providence Journal*, April 21, 2019, https://www.providencejournal.com/story/news/2019/04/22/civil-war-statue-on-marthas-vineyard-reopens-old-wounds/5378539007/.
147. Woollcott, *None but a Mule*, 137–38.
148. Lepore, "Why the School Wars Still Rage."

18. End of an Era

149. *Vineyard Gazette*, October 25, 1929.
150. *Vineyard Gazette*, February 17, 1928.
151. Ibid.
152. Ibid.
153. *Vineyard Gazette*, November 15, 1929.
154. West, *The Richer, The Poorer*, 239–40.
155. Pretsky, "Bringing the Great Depression."
156. Favreau, *Crash*, 57–58.
157. Ibid.
158. Wallance, "Despite Woes."
159. Railton, "Story of Martha's Vineyard."
160. West, *The Richer, The Poorer*, 240.
161. *Vineyard Gazette*, July 9, 1908.
162. *Vineyard Gazette*, May 26, 1933.
163. Railton, "Story of Martha's Vineyard."

BIBLIOGRAPHY

Allen, Everett. *Black Ships: Rumrunners of Prohibition*. Boston: Little, Brown and Company, 1979.

Baer, Chris. "Immigrants." *Martha's Vineyard Times*, January 31, 2017.

———. "Islands to Island." *Martha's Vineyard Times*, January 11, 2022.

———. "This Was Then: Razors, Shotguns, and Brass Knuckles." *Martha's Vineyard Times*, July 24, 2019.

Berry, Connie. "Have Faith: Traditions." *Martha's Vineyard Times*, January 18, 2022.

Brewster, Adam, and Caitlin Huey-Burns. "Proposals to Restrict Voting Gain Traction in Republican States." CBS News, February 25, 2021. https://www.cbsnews.com/news/voting-restriction-proposals-republican-states/.

Christiansen, Shelley. "The Shearer Family, Keepers of the Inn." *MV Magazine*, June 22, 2012. https://mvmagazine.com/news/2012/06/22/shearer-family-keepers-inn.

Cromwell, Adelaide. "The History of Oak Bluffs as a Popular Resort for Blacks." *Dukes County Intelligencer*, August 1984.

Currier, Geoff. "Let's Raise a Glass to Prohibition." Edible Vineyard, October 8, 2022. https://ediblevineyard.com/2020/10/08/lets-raise-glass-prohibition.

Dresser, Thomas. *African Americans of Martha's Vineyard*. Charleston, SC: The History Press, 2010.

———. *Hidden History of Martha's Vineyard*. Charleston, SC: The History Press, 2017.

———. *History of Martha's Vineyard*. Charleston, SC: The History Press, 2015.

———. *Music on Martha's Vineyard*. Charleston, SC: The History Press, 2014.

———. *The Rise of Tourism on Martha's Vineyard*. Charleston, SC: The History Press, 2020.

———. *Women of Martha's Vineyard*. Charleston, SC: The History Press, 2013.

Dunlop, Tom. "Historic Film Clips Reveal Edgartown in 1925." *Vineyard Gazette*, May 26, 2016.

Favreau, Marc. *Crash: The Great Depression and the Fall and Rise of America*. Boston: Little, Brown and Company, 2018.

Herman, Susan N. "Crystal Eastman, The ACLU's Underappreciated Founding Mother." ACLU, July 12, 2019. https://www.aclu.org/issues/free-speech/crystal-eastman-aclus-underappreciated-founding-mother.

Hufstader, Louisa. "Cronig's Celebrates 100 Years of Feeding the Vineyard Community." *Vineyard Gazette*, March 9, 2017.

———. "Still Learning at Want to Know Club." *Vineyard Gazette*, July 12, 2018.

Irmscher, Christoph. *Max Eastman: A Life*. New Haven, CT: Yale University Press, 2017.

Kolleth, Michael. "The Name Phillips Means Hardware." *Vineyard Gazette*, January 22, 1988.

Lee, Linsey. *More Vineyard Voices*. Edgartown, MA: Martha's Vineyard Historical Society, 2005.

———. *Vineyard Voices*. Edgartown, MA: Martha's Vineyard Historical Society, 1998.

———. *Vineyard Voices Three*. Vineyard Haven, MA: Martha's Vineyard Museum, 2019.

Lepore, Jill. "Why the School Wars Still Rage." *The New Yorker*, March 21, 2022.

Macmackin, Stuart. "From the Tivoli to the Ocean View." *Dukes County Intelligencer*, May 1983.

Meras, Phyllis. *Country Editor: Henry Beetle Hough and the Vineyard Gazette*. Bennington, VT: Images from the Past with the Martha's Vineyard Historical Society, 2008.

Myrick, Steve. "Sons of Gay Head Stood Strong in World War I." *Vineyard Gazette*, November 5, 2015.

Pretsky, Holly. "Bringing the Great Depression to Life for Young Adult Readers." *Vineyard Gazette*, May 10, 2018. https://vineyardgazette.com/news/2018/05/10/bringing-great-depression-life-young-adult-readers.

Railton, Arthur. "Craig Kingsbury." *Dukes County Intelligencer*, November 2004, 84–85.

———. *History of Martha's Vineyard: How We Got to Where We Are*. Beverly, MA: Commonwealth Editions in Association with Martha's Vineyard Historical Society, 2006.

———. "The Story of Martha's Vineyard: How We Got to Where We Are." *Dukes County Intelligencer*, November 2004.

———. "Tom Benton: Chilmarker." *Dukes County Intelligencer*, November 1989.

Richter, Annett Claudia. *Fiddles, Harmonicas and Banjos: Thomas Hart Benton and His Role in Constructing Popular Notions of American Folk Music and Musicians*. St. Paul: University of Minnesota Press, 2008.

Robards, Brooks. "'Annabell Lee' Shows Menemsha in the 1920s." *MV Times*, November 4, 2014. https://www.mvtimes.com/2014/11/04/annabelle-lee-shows-menemsha-1920s.

Scoville, Dorothy. *Shipwrecks on Martha's Vineyard*. Edgartown, MA: Dukes County Historical Society, 1991.

Scutts, Joanna. "How Crystal Eastman Fought for Equality." *The New Republic*, January 13, 2020. https://newrepublic.com/article/156180/crystal-eastman-fought-equality.

Shea, Jack. "Phillips Hardware: Old Values, New Ideas." *MV Times*, February 26, 2009.

Trotter, Mark. "IU's Eastman Residency in Martha's Vineyard." Indiana University–Bloomington. https://reei.indiana.edu/news-events/newsletter/archive/Spring%202020/IU%20Eastman%20Residency%20in%20Marthas%20Vineyard.html.

Wallance, Gregory. "Despite Woes, This Is No Great Depression." https://vineyardgazette.com/news/2012/04/19/despite-woes-no-great-depression.

Wallcox, Hilary, comp. "Gazette Chronicle: February 13, 1913." *Vineyard Gazette*, February 11, 2022.

———. "Gazette Chronicle: Snowbirds, March 11, 1927." *Vineyard Gazette*, March 11, 2022.

West, Dorothy. *The Richer, The Poorer*. New York: Doubleday, 1995.

Williamson, Miriam Huss. "The Singing 1920's." *Vineyard Gazette*, Friday August 3, 1979. https://vineyardgazette.com/news/1979/08/03/singing-1920s.

Wilson, Susan. "Information, Improvement, Sociability: The Triad Club." *Dukes County Intelligencer*, August 2007.

Wood, Cameron E., and Annie M. Wood. *Nomans Land*. New Bedford, MA: Reynolds Printing, 1931.

Woollcott, Barbara. *None but a Mule*. New York: Viking Press, 1944.

Periodicals

Dukes County Intelligencer (now *MV Quarterly*)

Martha's Vineyard Magazine

MV Times

New Yorker

New York Times

Vineyard Gazette

INDEX

AUTHOR'S NOTE

Author Thomas Dresser, with assistant Kutter, a miniature Schnauzer. *Photo by Joyce Dresser.*

This is my fifteenth book with The History Press and one of the more enjoyable to put together. I kept finding parallels between the 1920s and our current era. From politics to social customs to modern gadgets, we seem to be following similar patterns. Or perhaps it feels like we're living in a parallel universe.

Another element of pleasure I derived from this decade was the amount of historical information I could incorporate from previous books. The line of history may be twisted and full of curves, but the amount of information that can be translated from centuries, decades, years ago is important to set events in their proper perspective. Thus, I was able to draw on a vast amount of Vineyard history, which helps to present the present moment of the 1920s.

For fifteen years, I have authored these Vineyard histories. I'm getting long in the tooth, as the saying goes. I don't say I plan to stop writing, or even slow down, but simply take stock of where I am at this point in this career. I taught elementary school for a decade, I ran nursing homes for twenty years, I drove school and tour buses for a dozen years or so, but of all these occupational opportunities, writing is on top. I agree with Dorothy West's comment to Linsey Lee in *Vineyard Voices*: "I think writing is a compulsion. If you want to write, you just have to write. You know when I am the happiest is when I am writing. When I write something good, sometimes I get so happy my eyes just fill up with tears, sometimes I like what I wrote so much it brings a tear to my eye."

So, here I am. I recently turned seventy-six, happily ensconced with wife Joyce and our miniature Schnauzer, Kutter, living the life. We'll see what happens next…

Thomas Dresser, February 2023

For questions or comments, email me at thomasdresser@gmail.com

My website is thomasdresser.com.

And here are a few more books to enjoy:

African Americans of Martha's Vineyard
Disaster off Martha's Vineyard
Ghosts of Martha's Vineyard
Hidden History of Martha's Vineyard
Martha's Vineyard: A History
Martha's Vineyard in the American Revolution
Martha's Vineyard in World War II
Music on Martha's Vineyard
Mystery on the Vineyard
The Rise of Tourism on Martha's Vineyard
A Travel History of Martha's Vineyard
The Wampanoag Tribe of Martha's Vineyard
Whaling on Martha's Vineyard
Women of Martha's Vineyard